The Railroad Raiders

The Railroad Raiders

An Ohio Volunteers Recollections of the Andrews Raid to Disrupt the Confederate Railroad in Georgia During the American Civil War

William Pittenger

*The Railroad Raiders: an Ohio Volunteers Recollections of the
Andrews Raid to Disrupt the Confederate Railroad
in Georgia During the American Civil War*
by William Pittenger

Published by Leonaur Ltd

Text in this form copyright © 2007 Leonaur Ltd

ISBN: 978-1-84677-207-8 (hardcover)
ISBN: 978-1-84677-208-5 (softcover)

http://www.leonaur.com

Publisher's Note

The opinions expressed in this book are those of the author
and are not necessarily those of the publisher.

Contents

The Adventurers	9
Preface	11
Introduction	13
Mr Andrews' Audacious Enterprise	19
A Long Walk into Danger	25
Into the Heart of Rebeldom	30
How We Stole a Locomotive	35
The Great Railroad Chase	40
The Greatest Manhunt in the South	52
All Abandon Hope	59
Cast Into Cimmerian Gloom	69
Imprisonment & Escapes	79
Placed on Trial	90
Death Upon the Scaffold	96
Prisoner of the Confederacy	101
Our Bid for Freedom	108
I Assist a US Spy to Escape	116
Transported to the Rebel Capital	127
An Exchange is Proposed	136

The expedition, in the daring of its conception, had the wildness of a romance; while in the gigantic and overwhelming results it sought and was likely to accomplish, it was absolutely sublime.
Official Report of Hon. Judge Holt to the Secretary of War.

It was all the deepest laid scheme, and on the grandest scale, that ever emanated from the brains of any number of Yankees combined.
Atlanta "Southern Confederacy" of April 15th, 1862

The Adventurers

EXECUTED

J. J. Andrews, Leader		Citizen Of Kentucky
William Campbell		Citizen Of Kentucky
George D. Wilson	Co. B	Second Reg't Ohio Vols
Marion A. Ross	Co. A	Second Reg't Ohio Vols
Perry G. Shadrack	Co. K	Second Reg't Ohio Vols
Samuel Slavens		Thirty-Third Reg't Ohio Vols
Samuel Robinson	Co. G	Thirty-Third Reg't Ohio Vols
John Scott	Co. K	Twenty-First Reg't Ohio Vols

ESCAPED IN OCTOBER

W. W. Brown	Co. F	Twenty-First Reg't Ohio Vols
William Knight	Co. E	Twenty-First Reg't Ohio Vols
J. R. Porter	Co. C	Twenty-First Reg't Ohio Vols
Mark Wood	Co. C	Twenty-First Reg't Ohio Vols
J. A. Wilson	Co. C	Twenty-First Reg't Ohio Vols
M. J. Hawkins	Co. A	Thirty-Third Reg't Ohio Vols
John Wollam	Co. C	Thirty-Third Reg't Ohio Vols
D. A. Dorsey	Co. H	Thirty-Third Reg't Ohio Vols

EXCHANGED IN MARCH

Jacob Parrott	Co. K	Thirty-Third Reg't Ohio Vols
Robert Buffum	Co. H	Twenty-First Reg't Ohio Vols
William Bensinger	Co. G	Twenty-First Reg't Ohio Vols
William Reddick	Co. B	Thirty-Third Reg't Ohio Vols
E. H. Mason	Co. K	Twenty-First Reg't Ohio Vols
William Pittenger	Co. G	Second Reg't Ohio Vols

Preface

The following work is a narration of facts. My only desire is to give a clear and connected record of what will ever be regarded as a most remarkable episode in the history of the Great Rebellion.

The style of the book demands an apology. It was begun in sickness induced by the privations of rebel prisons, and completed amidst the fatigue and excitement of the most glorious campaign which has yet crowned our arms. Under these circumstances, there must be many faults of expression, which a generous reader will readily pardon.

To the many kind friends who sympathized with me during the weary interval when my fate was considered hopeless, as well as those who rejoiced with me on my return, I can only tender my most sincere thanks.

Myself and comrades are greatly indebted to the President and Secretary Stanton for their generous recognition of our services, and the munificent rewards bestowed upon us. To them, and to Judge Holt, Major-General Hitchcock, and James C. Wetmore, Ohio State Military Agent, we take this opportunity of expressing our heartfelt obligations.

Another to whom I am indebted is Dr. R. T. Trall of New York. At his beautiful *Hygiean Home*, on the mountain side, near Wernersville, Berks county, Pennsylvania, I regained my lost health. For his kindness, and that of his skilful assistants, Drs. Glass and Fairchild, I will ever be deeply grateful. It was with regret, woven with many pleasant memories, that I left their hospitable home when recovered health and duty called me again to the field.

To my early friend, Rev. Alexander Clark, Editor of the *School Visitor*, I am still more deeply indebted. His literary experience was freely placed at my service, and when discouraged in the preparation of my story, which was to me an arduous undertaking, his words of hope and cheer stimulated me to renewed efforts. But for aid derived from his sympathy and advice, I would have probably abandoned my task. May he be fully rewarded!

There are a host of others whose good offices will always be kindly remembered. Among them are W. R. Allison of the *Steubenville Herald*, Dr. John McCook, also of Steubenville, Dr. George McCook of Pittsburgh, Rev. William B. Watkins, A. M., Dr. John Mills, and many others. Thanks to them all!

William Pittenger
Army of the Cumberland, August, 1863

Introduction

While our absent brothers are battling on the field, it is becoming that the friends at home should be eager for the minutest particulars of the camp-life, courage and endurance of the dear boys far away; for to the loyal lover of his country every soldier is a brother.

The narrative related on the following pages is one of extraordinary "daring and suffering," and will excite an interest in the public mind such as has rarely, if ever, arisen from any personal adventures recorded on the page of history.

William Pittenger, the oldest of a numerous family, was born in Jefferson county, Ohio, January 31st, 1840. His father, Thomas Pittenger, is a farmer, and trains his children in the solid experiences of manual labour. His mother is from a thinking familyhood of people, many of whom are well known in Eastern Ohio as pioneers in social and moral progress—the Mills's. William learned to love his country about as early as he learned to love his own mother; for his first lessons were loyalty and liberty, syllabled by a mother's lips. Even before the boy could read, he knew in outline the history of our nation's trials and triumphs, from the days of Bunker Hill, forward to the passing events of the latest newspaper chronicling,—all of which facts were nightly canvassed around the cabin-hearth.

Although he was an adept in all branches of learning, yet, in school days, as now, young Pittenger had two favourite studies; and they happened to be the very ones in the prosecution of which his teachers could aid him scarcely at all—History and Astronomy. But, in the face of discouragement, with the aid only of accidental helps, and by the candle-light and the star-light after the sunny hours had been toiled away, he pressed patiently and perseveringly forward in his own chosen methods, until he became an accurate historian, and a practical astronomer. At the age of seventeen, he manufactured, for the most part with his own hands, a reflecting telescope, which his friends came from near and far to see, and gaze through, at the wonderful worlds unthought-of before.

The ambitions of farm-life were not sufficient to occupy the head and hands of this searcher for knowledge. To explore the fields of the firmament with his telescope, gave him intenser pleasure than the most faithful farmer ever realized from furrowing his fields in the dewiest spring mornings. To follow the footsteps of heroes through the world's annals, as they struggled up through conflicts to glorious liberty, thrilled him with a livelier enthusiasm than ever sprang from the music of marching harvesters. While other young men of his age and neighbourhood idled their rainy days and winter nights in trifling diversions, there was one who preferred the higher joy of communion with Humboldt in his *Cosmos*, Macaulay in his *England*, Irving in his *Columbus*, or Burritt in his *Geography of the Heavens*.

Owing to this decided preference for science and literature, the father found it advisable to indulge his son in the desire to enter a field more consonant with his wishes. He accordingly qualified himself, by close study at home, and without a tutor, for the profession of teaching. In this honourable avocation he laboured with industry and promise, until he felt constrained by love of country to quit the desk and the children, for the tent and the hosts of armed men.

During his career as teacher, he was, for awhile, associated with the writer in the publication of the *School Visitor*, then issued at Cleveland, Ohio. The enterprise was, at that time, (1857-8,) to the great outer world, an unnoticed and insignificant one; yet to those whose little all was enlisted in the mission of a Day School paper, it was, indeed, something that lay close upon their hearts. That was a cheerless, friendless time in the history of the little *Visitor*, to at least two inexperienced adventurers in the literary world. But these were hidden trials, and shall be unwritten still.

The never-forgotten teachings of his mother, together with the unconscious tuition resulting from observation and experience, made Pittenger an early and constant friend of freedom. Any mind imbued with an admiration of God's marches in the Heavens as an Omnipotent Creator, and inspired by a contemplation of God's finger in History as a merciful Deliverer, will rise to the high level of universal love to man, and will comprehend the broad equality of Gospel liberty and republican brotherhood. Let a man be educated, head and heart, and he will love freedom, and demand freedom, and "dare and suffer" for freedom, not for himself only, but for all the oppressed of the whole earth.

Reader, you may draw lines. You may profess a conservative Christianity that would theologize the very grace out of the command, "Love thy neighbour as thyself." You may ignore this Christ-like precept, and adopt something more fashionable and aristocratic; but if you do, you entertain in your heart treason, both to your Father in heaven and to your brother on earth. This law of love is revealed to lowly men. It cuts down through crowns and creeds and chains, and rests as a blessed benediction on sufferers and slaves. This is the inspiration that brings victory to our arms, and deals death to destroyers. This was the spirit that prompted our young hero to stand forth, one of the very first from his native county, a soldier for right and righteousness, the moment the Sumter cry rang up the valley of his Ohio home.

When Pittinger became a volunteer, it was for the suppression of the Rebellion with all its belongings,—and if its overthrow should tumble slavery, with its clanking fetters and howling hounds, to the uttermost destruction, he would grasp his gun the firmer for the hope, and thank God for the prospect, the test, and the toil! He enlisted as a soldier for his country, ready to march anywhere, strike with any weapon, endure any fatigue, or share any sorrow. He went out not merely an armoured warrior, to ward off attacks, not to strike off obnoxious top-growths; but to "lay the axe at the root of the tree," and to pierce the very heart of the monster iniquity.

In three days after the receipt of the startling intelligence that the Stars and Stripes had been fired upon by rebels in arms, Pittenger was on his way to the Capital as a private soldier in the Second Ohio Regiment of volunteers. He fought bravely on the disastrous 21st of July, in the battle of Bull Run, while many of his comrades fell bleeding at his side. For his calm, heroic conduct throughout that memorable day of peril and panic, he received the highest praise from every officer of his regiment. Although thus a sharer of war's sternest conflicts during the three months' campaign, he was ready to re-enlist immediately, when his country called for a longer service; and after a few days' rest beneath the old homestead roof, he was again on his way with the same regiment to the seat of war in the Southwest.

During the fall and winter he saw severe service on the "dark and bloody ground." No soldiers ever endured so many midnight marches more patiently, or manifested more self-sacrificing devotion to country, through rains and storms, and wintry desolations, than the noble Ohio Second, under the command of Colonel Harris, through the campaign in the mountains of eastern Kentucky.

In December, the regiment was transferred to the Division commanded by the lamented General Mitchel, then encamped at Louisville. From this point, the army pressed forward victoriously through Elizabethtown, Bowling Green, Nashville, and Murfreesboro', until the old banner floated in the Tennessee breezes at Shelbyville. While here, the daring expedition to penetrate the heart of the Confederacy was organized, of which party Pittenger was one of the most enthusiastic and determined.

From the day the brave fellows departed over the Southern hills on their adventurous journey, a veil was dropped which hid them from sight of friends for many weary months—and some of them for ever! No tidings came in answer to all the beseeching thought-questionings that followed their mysterious pathway "beyond the lines."

Vague rumours were current around the camp-fires and home-circles that the whole party had been executed. Friends began to despair. Strangers began to inquire as if for missing friends. A universal sympathy prevailed in their behalf, and whole communities were excited to the wildest fervour on account of the lost adventurers. The widely-read letters from the *Steubenville Herald's* army correspondent were missed, for Pittenger wrote no more. The family were in an agony of suspense for the silent, absent son and brother. His ever faithful friend, Chaplain Gaddis, of the Ohio Second, made an effort to go, under a flag of truce, in search of the party, but was dissuaded by the commanding officers from so hopeless an undertaking. The summer passed, and yet no tidings came. The autumn came with its melancholy,—and uncertain rumours, like withered, fallen leaves, were again afloat about the camps and the firesides. The dreary winter came, and still the hearts of the most hopeful were chilled with disappointment. The father began to think of William as dead,—the mother to talk of her darling as one who had lived,—the children to speak of their elder brother as one they should never see any more until all the lost loved ones meet in the better land. The writer was even solicited by a mutual friend to preach the funeral sermon of one whose memory was still dear, but whom none of us ever hoped to see again on earth.

But our Father in heaven was kinder than we thought. Our prayers had been heard! As our fervent petitions winged up from family altars to the ear of the Infinite Lover, the guardian angels winged afar downward through battle alarms, and ministered to him for whom we besought protection. When the bright spring days came smiling over the earth, a message came from the hand of the missing one, brighter and sunnier to our hearts than the April sunlight on the hills! Soon the story was told, and we all thanked God for the merciful deliverance of him for whom we prayed, and who had found, even in a dismal prison-cell, the Pearl of great price! The one we loved returned home a witness of the Spirit that came to him as a Comforter in his dreariest loneliness, and is already a minister of the precious Gospel that gladdened him in the time of his tribulation.

And now the reader shall know all about the tedious delay and the long silence, from the pen of him who survives to tell the story.

We commend to all who peruse this narrative an interesting volume, entitled *Beyond the Lines*, another sad rehearsal of terror in rebel prisons and Southern swamps, in other portions of the Confederacy—the experience of Rev. Capt. J. J. Geer, now one of Lieutenant Pittenger's associate-advocates for liberty in the pulpit, as he was recently a brother-bondman in the land of tyranny and death.

A. C.
Philadelphia, September 15, 1863

Chapter 1
Mr Andrews' Audacious Enterprise

It is painful for me to write the adventures of the last year. As I compose my mind to the task, there arises before me the memory of days of suffering, and nights of sleepless apprehension—days and nights that, in their black monotony, seemed well nigh eternal. And the sorrow, too, which I felt on that terrible day, when my companions, whom common dangers and common sufferings had made as brothers to me, were dragged away to an ignominious death that I expected soon to share—all comes before me in the vividness of present reality, and I almost shrink back and lay down the pen. But I believe it to be a duty to give to the public the details of the great railroad adventure, which created such an excitement in the South, and which Judge Holt pronounced to be the most romantic episode of the war, both on account of the intrinsic interest involved, and still more because of the light it throws on the manners and feelings of the Southern people, and their conduct during the rebellion.

With this view, I have decided to give a detailed history of the expedition, its failure, and the subsequent imprisonment and fate of all of the members of the party. In doing this, I will have the aid of the survivors of the expedition—fourteen in all—and hope to give a narrative that will combine the strictest truth with all the interest of a romance.

In order to understand why the destruction of the Georgia State Railroad was of so much consequence, I will refer to the situation of affairs in the Southwest, in the opening of the spring of 1862.

The year commenced very auspiciously for our arms. Fort Donelson had fallen, after a desperate contest, and nearly all its garrison were taken prisoners. The scattered remains of the rebel army, under Johnston, had retreated precipitately from Kentucky, which had indeed been to them "the dark and bloody ground." Columbus and Nashville were evacuated, and fell into our hands. Island No. 10 was invested, and the Tennessee river groaned beneath a mighty army afloat, the same that had conquered Donelson, under its popular leader, General Grant, and which, it was fondly hoped, would strike far away into the centre of the rebel States. Throughout the North, men talked of the war as done, and speculated as to the terms of a peace that was soon to come.

But the end was not yet. The rebel leaders, who had embarked their all in this cause, and had pictured to themselves a magnificent slaveholding empire, stretching away from the Potomac to the Sierra Madre, in Mexico, and swallowing up all tropical America in one mighty nation, devoted to the interests of cotton and slavery alone, over which they should reign, were not yet satisfied to relinquish their cause as desperate, and abandon their glorious dreams. With a wonderful energy that must command our admiration, though it be only of the kind that is accorded to Satan as pictured in "Paradise Lost," they passed the conscription law, abandoned the posts they still held on the frontier, and concentrated their forces on a shorter line of defence.

The eastern part of this line extended from Richmond, through Lynchburg, to East Tennessee. In the west, it was represented by the Memphis and Charleston Railroad, extending from Memphis, through Corinth, Huntsville, Chattanooga, and Atlanta, to Charleston. Here they poured forward their new levies, and began to prepare for another desperate contest.

The unaccountable inertness of the Eastern army of the Union, under McClellan, gave them time to strengthen their defences, and reinforce their army, which had dwindled to a very low ebb during the winter. But while the commander of the East was planning strategy that, by the slowness of its development, if by nothing *worse*, was destined to dim the lustre of the Union triumphs, and lose the results of a year of war, the West was in motion. Down the Mississippi swept our invincible fleet, with an army on shore to second its operations. Up the Tennessee steamed Grant's victorious army, and Buell, with forty thousand men, was marching across the State of Tennessee, to reach the same point. My own division, under the lamented General O. M. Mitchel, was also marching across the State, but in a different direction, having Chattanooga as its ultimate aim, while Morgan, with another strong force, many of whom were refugees from East Tennessee, lay before Cumberland Gap, ready to strike through that fastness to Knoxville, and thus reach the very heart of rebellion.

To meet these powerful forces, whose destination he could not altogether foresee, Beauregard, who commanded in the west, concentrated his main army at Corinth, with smaller detachments scattered along the railroad to Chattanooga. The railroads on which he relied for supplies and reinforcements, as well as for communication with the eastern portion of rebeldom, formed an irregular parallelogram, of which the northern side extended from Memphis to Chattanooga, the eastern from Chattanooga to Atlanta, the southern from Atlanta to Jackson, Mississippi, and the western, by a network of roads, from Jackson to Memphis. The great East Tennessee and Virginia Railroad, which has not inaptly been called "the backbone of the rebellion," intersected this parallelogram at Chattanooga. Thus it will be seen that to destroy the northern and eastern sides of this parallelogram isolated Beauregard, and left East Tennessee, which was then almost stripped of troops, to fall easily before General Morgan.

So important was this destruction of communication deemed by those in power, that it was at first intended to reach both sides, and destroy them by armies; but the distance was so great that the design of destroying it in this manner was abandoned.

However, just at this time, J. J. Andrews, who was a secret agent of the United States, and had repeatedly visited every part of the South, proposed another method of accomplishing the same object, by means of a *secret* military expedition, to burn the bridges on the road, and thus interrupt communication long enough for the accomplishment of the schemes which were expected to give rebellion in the south-west its death-blow. He first made the proposition to General Buell, who did not, for some reason, approve of it. Afterwards he repeated it to General Mitchel, who received it with more favour.

Our division was at this time lying at Murfreesboro', repairing some bridges that had been destroyed, preparatory to an onward march further into the interior. All at once, eight men were detailed from our regiment—four of them from my own company. No one knew anything of their object or destination, and numberless were the conjectures that were afloat concerning them. Some supposed they had gone home to arrest deserters; others, that they were deserters themselves. But this last idea was contradicted by the fact that they were seen in close and apparently confidential communication with the officers just before their departure, as well as by the character of the men themselves, who were among the boldest and bravest of the regiment. Many supposed that they were sent into the enemy's country as spies; but the idea of sending such a number of spies from the privates in the ranks was so obviously absurd, that I did not seriously consider it. However, I was not long to remain in uncertainty, for an officer, who was an intimate friend of mine, revealed the secret to me. The enterprise was so grand and so audacious, that it instantly charmed my imagination, and I at once went to Colonel L. A. Harris, of the Second Ohio, and asked, as a favour from him, that if any detail was made for another expedition of the same kind, I should be placed on it.

Soon after, one of the party, from Company C, returned, and reported that he had ventured as far as Chattanooga, and there had met a Confederate soldier who recognized him as belonging to the Union army; and while, for the sake of old friendship, he hesitated to denounce him to the authorities, yet advised him to return, which he immediately did, and arrived safely in camp in a few days. He would give no details that might embarrass his companions, who were still pressing their way onward into the Confederacy.

A short time after this, all the party came back, and I received full details of their trip to the centre of rebeldom. They had proceeded in citizens' dress, on foot and unsuspected, to Chattanooga; there had taken the cars for Atlanta, where they arrived in safety. Here they expected to meet a Georgia engineer, who had been running on the State road for some time, and, with his assistance, intended to seize the passenger train, at breakfast, and run through to our lines, burning all the bridges in their rear. For several days they waited for him, but he came not. They afterwards learned that he had been pressed to run troops to Beauregard, who was then concentrating every available man at Corinth, in anticipation of the great battle which afterwards took place. Thus foiled, and having no man among them capable of running an engine, they abandoned the enterprise for that time, and quietly stole back to our lines. Had an engineer then been along, they would, in all probability, have been successful, as the obstacles which afterward defeated us did not then exist.

Our camp had been moved onward from Murfreesboro' to Shelbyville, which is a beautiful little city, situated on Duck river. We camped above the town, in a delightful meadow.

It was Sabbath, the 6th of April, and the earliness of the clime made the birds sing, and the fields bloom with more than the brilliancy of May in our own northern land. Deeply is the quiet of that Sabbath, with the green beauty of the warm spring landscape, pictured on my mind! An impression, I know not what, made me devote the day to writing letters to my friends. It was well I did so, for long and weary months passed ere I was permitted to write to them again.

But while the day was passing in such sweet repose with us, it was far different in another army; that was the day on which Grant was surprised by Beauregard, and only saved from destruction by the assistance of the gunboats. This, however, we did not learn for several days after.

On Monday, Andrews returned to our camp. He had spent some time along the line of the Georgia State road, and on his return reported to General Mitchel that the scheme was still feasible, and would be of more advantage than ever. He, however, asked for a larger detail of men, and twenty-four were given from the three Ohio regiments then in Sill's Brigade. One man was detailed from a company, though all the companies were not represented, and I believe in two[1] instances, two men were detailed from one company—they were probably intimate friends, who wished to go together.

During the day, I saw Andrews in the camp. I had seen him frequently before, away up in the mountains of eastern Kentucky, but did not then observe him particularly. Now I paid more attention. He was nearly six feet in height, of powerful frame, black hair, and long, black, silken beard, Roman features, a high and expansive forehead, and a voice fine and soft as a woman's. He gave me the impression of a man who combined intellect and refinement with the most cool and dauntless courage. Yet his manner and speech, which was slow and pensive, indicated what I afterwards found to be almost his only fault—a slowness to decide on the spur of the moment, and back his decision by prompt, vigorous action. This did not detract from his value as a secret agent, when alone, for then all his actions were premeditated, and carried out with surpassing coolness and bravery; but it did unfit him for the command of men, in startling emergencies, where instant action afforded the only chance of safety. This trait of character will be more fully developed in the course of my story. I conversed with him on the object of the expedition, not, of course, expecting a full detail, but receiving a general idea. I put particular stress on his promise, that whatever happened, he would keep us all together, and, if necessary, we would cut our way through in a body. This was because, being near-sighted, and, therefore, a bad hand to travel in a strange country, with no guide, I had a particular horror of being left alone.

I returned to my company, and procured a suit of citizen's clothes from our boys who had been out before. All the members of the company, seeing me so arrayed, came around to try to dissuade me from

---

1. One of these I noticed only very lately.

the enterprise, which to them appeared full of unknown perils. It was gratifying to be the object of so much solicitude, but having decided to go, I could not yield.

My captain, J. F. Sarratt, of Company G, Second Ohio, as brave and true-hearted a soldier as ever lived, earnestly entreated me not to go; but finding my determination was fixed, he bade me an affectionate farewell. Seldom have I parted with more emotion from any one than these war-worn veterans.

It was about four o'clock in the afternoon when we left camp, and started for the place of rendezvous at Shelbyville. The sun was shining brightly, and the bracing evening air sent the blood coursing cheerily through our veins, and inspired us with the brightest hopes of the future. Soon we reached Shelbyville, and lingered there for an hour or two, when Ross and I, acting under the previous direction of Andrews, started out of town. Our orders were for us all to proceed along the road in small squads, for two or three miles, and then halt and wait for him.

We walked quietly along, until about dark, when, seeing none of the others, we began to grow uneasy, fearing we had gone on the wrong road. We met several persons, but they could give no account of any one before; then we saw a house just by the road, and crossing the fence, went up to it to get a drink of water. Before we reached the door, a dog came up behind my companion and bit him—then ran away before punishment could be inflicted.

The bite was not severe, and I good-humouredly laughed at his mishap; but before we again reached the fence, the same dog came once more. Ross saw him, and sprang over the fence; but I had only time to reach the top of it, where I sat in fancied security. But the merciless whelp, in his ire, sprang at me, seized my coat, and tore a large piece out of it! That coat, thus *cur*-tailed, I wore all through Dixie. I mention this incident, because it was what some would call a bad omen.

Chapter 2

A Long Walk into Danger

We now proceeded on our way—not rejoicing, for our situation grew every moment more perplexing. Darkness was falling rapidly, and not one of our comrades was visible. We were almost certain we had taken the wrong road. Finally, we resolved to retrace our steps, and endeavour to obtain some clue to our journey, or if we could not, to return to camp; for, without instruction, we knew not how or where to go. We therefore retraced our steps till in sight of Shelbyville, and then, sure that none could pass without our knowledge, we waited nearly an hour longer.

Our patience was rewarded. A few, whom we recognized as belonging to our party, came along the road; we fell in with them, and were soon overtaken by others, among whom was Andrews. Now all was right. Soon we were as far from Shelbyville as Ross and I had been when alone, and a few hundred yards further on we found the remainder of our comrades.

In a little thicket of dead and withered trees, sufficiently open to assure us that no listening ear was near, we halted, and Andrews revealed to us his plans. There were twenty-three gathered around him; twenty-four had been detailed, but from some cause, one had failed to report. In low tones, amid the darkness, he gave us the details of the romantic expedition.

We were to break up in small squads of three or four, and travel as far south as Chattanooga. If questioned, we were to answer so as to avoid exciting suspicion, and tell any plausible tale that might answer our purpose.

We were to travel rapidly, and, if possible, reach Chattanooga on Thursday evening at five o'clock. This was Monday, and the distance was one hundred and three miles, a heavy travel on foot; but then we were allowed to hire conveyances, if we could.

Andrews then gave us some Confederate money to bear our expenses, and we parted. There were three others with me; P. G. Shadrack, of Company K, Second Ohio, a merry, reckless fellow, but at heart noble and generous; William Campbell, a citizen of Kentucky, who had received permission to come with us, in a soldier's place. He was a man of two hundred and twenty pounds weight, handsome as Apollo, and of immense physical strength, which he was not slow to use when roused, though good-natured and clever in the main.

The third was the most remarkable man of the whole party. He was not educated highly, though he had read a great deal; but in natural shrewdness, I rarely, if ever, saw his equal. He had travelled extensively over the United States, had observed everything, and remembered all he observed. Had he lived, the composition of this book would have been in abler hands than mine. In addition to this, he excelled, perhaps, even Parson Brownlow, in the fiery and scorching denunciation he could hurl on the head of an opponent. In action he was brave and cool; no danger could frighten him, no emergency find him unprepared. These were my companions.

The rain had begun to fall slightly as we walked out the railroad, on our route, and soon it increased to torrents. The night was pitchy dark, and we stumbled along, falling into gutters here, and nearly sticking in the mud there, until midnight, when we resolved to seek shelter from the storm.

For a long time we could find no indication of a house, until, at last, the barking of a dog gave us a clue. After some dispute as to which side of the road it was on, we struck off over a field. Our only guide were the random flashes of lightning that gave us a momentary view of the country around. The better to prosecute our search, we formed a line within hearing distance of each other, and thus swept around in all directions. At last we found a barn, but were so wet and chilly that we resolved to hunt on, in the hope of finding a fire and a bed.

After a still more tedious search, we found the goal of our wishes. It was a rude, double log-house. Here we roused up the inmates, and demanded a shelter for the night. The man of the house was evidently alarmed, but let us in, and then commenced questioning us as to who we were.

We told him we were Kentuckians who were disgusted with the tyranny of the Lincoln Government, and were seeking an asylum in the free and independent South.

"Oh," said he, "you come on a bootless errand, and had better go back home, for I have no doubt the whole of the South will soon be as much under Lincoln as Kentucky is."

"Never!" we answered, "we will fight till we die first!"

At this the old man chuckled quietly, and only said, "Well, we'll see; we'll see," which closed the discussion.

We were truly glad to find a Union man under such circumstances, but did not dare to reveal our true character to him, and he probably believes to this day that he harboured some chivalric Southerners. However, he provided us with a good supper and a comfortable bed, promising, also, not to inform the Federal pickets on us. The next morning, the sky for a time was clear, but it soon became overcast, and we were again compelled to suffer the inevitable drenching that befell us every day of this dreary journey.

We reached Wartrace in the midst of a pelting storm. At first we intended to go around the town, as it was the last station on our picket line. It was raining so hard that we thought we would not be interrupted in passing through it, but our guards were too vigilant for us. They stopped us, and after being for some time detained, and trying to play off the innocent Southern citizen, as hundreds do, we were obliged to reveal our true character to the commanding officer of the post, which, of course, secured our release.

Then again, we travelled onward for a time, wading the swollen creeks, and plodding through the mud as fast as we could. We were now outside of our lines, with nothing to trust to but the tender mercies of the rebels. Soon after, we found what a slender ground of trust that was, but *now* we were safe in the completeness of our disguise.

We met many others of our party, and trudged along—sometimes in company with them, but oftener alone. Toward evening, we reached Manchester, crossed Duck river, which was at flood height, and entered the town.

Here we found the population in a wild ferment, and on inquiring the cause, learned that some of the citizens had reported an approaching band of Yankee cavalry, and that they were even now visible from the public square. We repaired thither with all speed to witness the novel spectacle of the entrance of National troops into a hostile town, from a Southern point of view. Mingled were the emotions expressed; fear was most prominent, but I thought I could detect on some countenances a half-concealed smile of exultation. Soon the terrible band loomed up over the hill which bounded the view, when lo! the dreaded enemies were seen to be only a party of negroes, who had been working in the coal mines in the mountains somewhere. Some of Mitchel's men had destroyed the works, and the contrabands were brought here for safe keeping. The feelings of the chivalry may be better imagined than described, as they dispersed with curses on the whole African race!

We here obtained from some of the citizens the names of the most prominent secessionists along the route we were to travel, who would be most likely to help us on to that blissful land where we might enjoy our rights in peace undisturbed by even dreams of Abolitionists. These names were a great advantage to us, because always having some one to inquire for, and being recommended from one influential man to another, it was taken for granted that we were trustworthy characters, and few questions asked. That night we were within a few miles of Hillsboro', but so much were we delayed by the rain, that we began to fear we could not reach our destination in time. My feet, too, were sore from the gravel and dirt that filled my shoes in crossing the creeks, and wading through the mud, and already we were weary and stiff from travelling in the wet. But we resolved to press on, and, if necessary, to travel in the night, too, rather than miss our appointment.

Where we stayed that night, I first heard from the lips of a slave-owner himself of hunting negroes with bloodhounds. Our host said he had seen some one dodging around the back of his plantation, by the edge of the woods, just as it was getting dark, and in the morning he would take his bloodhounds, and go to hunt him up, and if it proved to be a negro, he would get the reward. He said he had caught great numbers of them, and seemed to regard it as a highly profitable business.

We, of course, had to agree with him; but I well remember that the idea of hunting human beings with bloodhounds, for money, sent a thrill of horror and detestation through my veins. Not long after, we found that bloodhounds were not for negroes alone.

The next morning, we continued our journey, and after walking three miles, found a man who agreed, for an exorbitant price, and for the good of the Confederacy, to give us conveyance in a wagon for a few miles. This was a great help to us, and as we trotted briskly along, we soon came in sight of the Cumberland Mountains.

Never did I behold more beautiful scenery. The rain had for a short time ceased to fall, and the air was clear. The mountains shone in the freshest green, and around their tops, just high enough to veil their loftiest summits, clung a soft, shadowy mist, gradually descending lower, shrouding one after another of the spurs and high mountain valleys from view. But the beautiful scene did not long continue. Soon the mist deepened into cloud, and again the interminable rain began to fall. To add to our discomforts, our wagon would go no further, and once more we trudged along afoot.

At noon we stopped for dinner at a house belonging to one of the "sand-hillers." This is the general name applied to the poor class of whites at the South. They have no property of their own, and live in small hovels, on the worst portions of the lands of the rich. Here they lead an ignorant, lazy life, devoting most of their time to hunting and fishing; only raising a little patch of corn to furnish their bread. They are almost as completely owned by their landlords as the slaves, and are compelled to vote as their masters choose. In the social scale they are no higher than any slave, nor do they deserve to be, for their intelligence is less. The term "sand-hiller," or "clay-eater," is a terrible one of reproach, and is applied unsparingly by the aristocrats. Of course, our entertainment here was composed of rather rude fare, but we ate the half-ground and half-baked corn bread, with the strong pork, and went on our way rejoicing.

Chapter 3

Into the Heart of Rebeldom

We were near the foot of the Cumberland Mountains, and addressed ourselves to the task of crossing them. Just as we were mounting the first spur, we fell in with a Confederate soldier, who was at home on a furlough. He had been in a number of battles, and among others the first Manassas, which he described very minutely to me. Little did he think that I, too, had been there, as we laughed together at the wild panic of the Yankees. He was greatly delighted to see so many Kentuckians coming out on the right side, and contrasted our noble conduct with that of some persons of his own neighbourhood, who still sympathized with the Abolitionists.

When we parted, he grasped my hand with tears in his eyes, and said he hoped "the time would soon come when we would be comrades, fighting side by side in one glorious cause." My heart revolted from the hypocrisy I was compelled to use; but having commenced, there was no possibility of turning back.

On we clambered up the mountain till the top was reached; then across the summit, which was a tolerably level road for six miles; then down again, over steep rocks, yawning chasms, and great gullies; a road that none but East Tennesseeans or soldier Yankees could have travelled at all. This rough jaunt led us down into Battle Creek, which is a delightful, picturesque valley, hemmed in by projecting ridges of lofty mountains.

While here, they told me how this valley obtained its name, which is certainly a very romantic legend, and no doubt true.

In early times there was war among the Indians. One tribe made a plundering expedition into the camp of another, and after securing their booty retreated. Of course they were pursued, and in their flight were traced to this valley. There the pursuers believed them to be concealed, and to make their capture sure, divided their force into two bands, each one taking an opposite side of the valley.

It was early in the morning, and as they wended their way cautiously onward, the mountain mist came down just as I had seen it descend that morning, and enveloped each of the parties in its folds. Determined not to be foiled, they marched on, and meeting at the head of the valley, each supposed the other to be the enemy. They poured in their fire, and a deadly conflict ensued. Not till nearly all their number had fallen did the survivors discover their mistake, and they slowly and sorrowfully returned to their wigwams. The plunderers, who had listened to their conflict in safety, being further up the mountains, were thus left to carry home their booty in triumph.

But we had no leisure for legendary tales.

The sun had set, and we stopped for the night with a rabid Secessionist, whom our soldier-friend on the mountain had recommended to us. He received us with open arms, shared with us the best his house afforded—giving us his bedroom, and sleeping with his family in the kitchen. We spent the evening in denouncing the Abolitionists, which term was used indiscriminately to designate all Federals who did not advocate the acknowledgment of the Confederacy. This did not go quite so hard as it did at first, for practice had rendered it nearly as easy for us to falsify our sentiments as to express them plainly.

Among other things we instanced to show the tyranny of the Lincolnites in Kentucky, was the expatriation law. This law provides that all persons aiding or abetting the rebels, or leaving the State and going South with their army, shall be *expatriated*, and lose all their right of citizenship in the State. The old man thought this was an act of unparalleled oppression; and in the morning, before I was out of bed, came in the room, and desired that some one of us would write that law down, that he might show his Union neighbours what the Yankees would do when they had the sway. I wrote it, and we all afterward signed our names to it. No doubt that document has been the theme of many angry discussions.

So thoroughly did we deceive the old man, that when, three days after, the railroad adventure fell on the astonished Confederates like a clap of thunder out of a clear sky, he would not believe that we were part of the men engaged in it. One of his neighbours, who was a Union man, and was arrested and confined in the same prison with us, told us that to the last our host maintained that his guests, at least, were true and loyal Southerners. Should I ever again be in that part of the country, I would delight to call on him in my true character, and talk over the national troubles from another point of view.

We stayed with him Wednesday night, and were still a long way from Chattanooga. We had designed, notwithstanding our weariness, to travel all that night, but accidentally met some of our comrades who had seen Andrews, who informed them that he had postponed the enterprise one day longer. This was a great relief, as it saved us a most wearisome and dreaded night tramp. But better to have taken it, for the delay of that *one* day was fatal. On Friday there would have been no extra trains to meet, and our success would have been sure. But this we did not know at the time.

The next day, which was Thursday, we came to Jasper, stopped in the town and around the groceries awhile, talking of the state of the country. We told them Kentucky was just ready to rise and shake off her chains, and they were just foolish enough to believe it!

Here we heard the first indistinct rumour of the battle of Shiloh—of course, a wonderful victory to the rebels, killing thousands of Yankees, and capturing innumerable cannon. It was the impression that our army was totally destroyed. One countryman gravely assured me that five hundred gunboats had been sunk. I told him I did not think the Yankees had so many as that, but was unable to shake his faith.

That night we stayed at Widow Hall's, and there met Andrews and some of our other comrades. This was on the banks of the Tennessee river, and Andrews advised us to cross there, and to take passage on the cars at Shell Mound station, as there had been a stringent order issued to let no one cross above, who could not present perfectly satisfactory credentials. Andrews had these, but we had not; it was, therefore, advisable for us to be challenged as few times as possible. We passed a pleasant evening, during which the wit of my friend Shadrack kept us in a continual roar of laughter.

At last morning came, and we went down to the bank of the river to cross. The ferryman had just swung the boat into the stream, and we were getting into it, when a man arrived with positive orders from the military authorities to let no one across for three days.

Affairs now looked dark. We could not cross except at the upper ferries, and not there unless our credentials were good. However, we resolved to persevere, and thinking in this case, as in many others, the boldest plan would be the safest, we again struck over the wild spurs of the Cumberland, which here sweep directly down to the river, on in the direction of Chattanooga, with the intention of trying to cross there, at headquarters.

Our journey was far from a pleasant one, and several times we lost our road in the entanglements of the mountains; but at last we reached a valley that ran directly down to the river, opposite Chattanooga.

Here the road was more frequented, and from the travellers we met we learned further particulars of the battle of Shiloh. Still the accounts were rose-tinted for the Confederates, though they now admitted a considerable loss.

One man gave me an interesting item of news from the East; it was, that the Merrimac had steamed out, and after engaging the Monitor for some time with no decisive results, had ran alongside, and throwing grappling-hooks on her, towed her ashore, where, of course, she fell an easy prey. He said that now they had the two best gunboats in the world, and they would be able to raise the blockade without difficulty, and even to burn the Northern cities. But I have not space to tell of all the wild chimeras and absurd stories that we heard on our entrance into a land where truth always has been contraband. From that time forward, we heard of continuous Confederate victories, and not one Union triumph, till in September, when they admitted that they were repulsed by Rosecrans at Corinth.

On reaching the river, we found a great number of persons on the bank waiting to go over. The ferryman was there with a horse-boat, but the wind was so high that he feared to attempt the crossing. We waited as patiently as we could, though the time for the cars to start on the other side had nearly arrived, and we could not well afford to miss them. At length, the ferryman agreed to attempt the passage. He found it very difficult. We were about an hour in crossing, though the river was only a few hundred yards in width. Several times we were beaten back to our own side, but at last perseverance conquered, and we landed at Chattanooga.

The passage was an anxious one, for we expected to find the guard waiting for us on the other side; and then, if we failed to satisfy them that we were loyal subjects of King Jefferson, we would at once land in a Southern prison. Judge, then, of our delight when we saw no guard there, and were permitted to pass unmolested and unquestioned on our route.

I do not yet know the reason of this sudden relaxation of vigilance. Perhaps it was because all their attention was directed to Huntsville, which was now occupied in force by General Mitchel. The panic produced by this occupation was immense, as the only communication it left them with Beauregard was by the circuitous route through Atlanta, and when, the next day, this too was endangered, their excitement knew no bounds.

Chattanooga is a small town—not much more than a village. It is pleasantly situated on the banks of the Tennessee, and is bowered in amidst lofty mountain peaks. One of these hangs right over the town, and is more than seven hundred feet in perpendicular height. From its summit parts of four States are visible—Tennessee, Georgia, Alabama, and North Carolina. It is capable of being very strongly fortified; and though there were no works erected when I was there, many may have been built since. It is one of the most important strategic points in the whole South, and should have been in the possession of our forces long ago.

From the river we went directly to the depot. Some of our party had arrived earlier, and gone down to Marietta on a former train. We found the cars nearly ready to start, and after loitering around a few minutes in the depot, which was crowded full of travellers—mostly soldiers—we purchased our tickets and got aboard. The cars were jammed full. There was scarcely room to stand. Many of the passengers were soldiers who had been at home on furlough, and were returning to join Beauregard. The conversation was mostly on the great battle which had just been fought, and the accounts were by no means so glowing as they had been at first; still they announced a great victory. We took part in the conversation, and expressing as much interest as any one, our true character was not suspected. There was at this time no system of passports in use on that line, and travel was entirely unrestricted.

The sun was about an hour high as we glided out of the depot, and soon sunk to rest behind the hills of Georgia. There were many bridges on the road, and as we passed over them, we could not help picturing to ourselves our proposed return on the morrow, and the probabilities of the destruction we intended to wreck on them. Darkness gradually closed in, and on we went amid the laughter and oaths of the Confederates, many of whom were very much intoxicated. I procured a seat on the coal-box, and for awhile gave myself up to the reflections naturally suggested by the near culmination of the enterprise in which I was engaged. Visions of former days and friends—dear friends, both around the camp-fire and by the hearth of home, whom I might never see again, floated before me. But gradually, as the night wore on, these faded, and I slept.

At midnight, we were wakened by the conductor calling "Marietta." The goal was reached. We were in the centre of the Confederacy, with our deadly enemies all around. Before we left, we were to strike a blow that would either make all rebeldom vibrate to the centre, or be ourselves at the mercy of the merciless. It was a time for solemn thought; but we were too weary to indulge in speculations of the future. We retired to bed in the Tremont House, and were soon folded in sweet slumbers—the last time we slept on a bed for many weary months.

Chapter 4

How We Stole a Locomotive

The waiter aroused us at four o'clock in the morning, as we told him we wished to take the train at that hour back to Camp McDonald, which is located at a place called Big Shanty, eight miles north of Marietta, and is also a breakfast station. Andrews had gone to another hotel, and warned the members of the party there to be in readiness to take passage. Two of them, Hawkins and Porter, who had arrived earlier, were not warned, and were, therefore, left behind. It was not their fault, as they had no certain knowledge of the time we were to start, but rather thought it would be the next day.

There were just twenty of us on the train, Andrews and nineteen others, of whom several were engineers. We went along very quietly and inoffensively, just as any other passengers would do, until we reached Big Shanty. I knew that we were to take possession of the train at this place, but did not just know how it was to be done. I thought we would probably have to fight, and compel the conductor, train-hands, and passengers to get off. We might have done this, but it would have required very quick work, for there were then some ten thousand troops, mostly conscripts, camped there, and a guard was placed watching the train. But a far better plan was adopted.

As soon as we arrived, the engineer, conductor, and many of the passengers went over to the eating-house. Now was our opportunity! Andrews, and one or two others, went forward and examined the track, to see if everything was in readiness for a rapid start.

Oh! what a thrilling moment was that! Our hearts throbbed thick and fast with emotions we dared not manifest to those who were loafing indifferently around. In a minute, which seemed an hour, Andrews came back, opened the door, and said, very quietly and carelessly, "Let us go, now, boys." Just as quietly and carelessly we arose and followed him. The passengers who were lazily waiting for the train to move on and carry them to their destination, saw nothing in the transaction to excite their suspicions. Leisurely we moved forward—reached the head of the train—then Andrews, Brown our engineer, and Knight, who also could run an engine, leaped on the locomotive; Alfred Wilson took the top of the cars as brakesman, and the remainder of us clambered into the foremost baggage car, which, with two others, had been previously uncoupled from the hinder part of the train. For one moment of most intense suspense all was still—then a pull—a jar—a clang—and we were flying away on our perilous journey.

There are times in the life of man when whole years of intensest enjoyment seem condensed into a single moment. It was so with me then. I could comprehend the emotion of Columbus, when he first beheld through the dim dawn of morning, the new found, but long dreamed-of shores of America, or the less innocent, but no less vivid joy of Cortez, when he first planted the cross of Spain over the golden halls of Montezuma. My breast throbbed full with emotions of delight and gladness, that words labour in vain to express. A sense of ethereal lightness ran through all my veins, and I seemed to be ascending higher—higher—into realms of inexpressible bliss, with each pulsation of the engine. It was a moment of triumphant joy that will never return again. Not a dream of failure now shadowed my rapture. All had told us that the greatest difficulty was to reach and take possession of the engine, and after that, success was certain. *It would have been*, but for unforeseen contingencies.

Away we scoured, passing field, and village, and woodland. At each leap of the engine our hearts rose higher, and we talked merrily of the welcome that would greet us when we dashed into Huntsville a few hours later—our enterprise done, and the brightest laurels of the guerrilla Morgan far eclipsed!

But the telegraph ran by our side, and was able, by the flashing of a single lightning message ahead, to arrest our progress and dissipate all our fondest hopes. There was no telegraphic station where we took the train, but we knew not how soon our enemies might reach one, or whether they might not have a portable battery at command. To obviate all danger on this point, we stopped, after running some four miles, to cut the wire.

John Scott, an active young man, climbed the pole, and with his hand knocked off the insulated box at the top, and swung down on the wire. Fortunately, there was a small saw on the engine, with which the wire was soon severed. While this was being done, another party took up a rail, and put it into the car to carry off with us. This did not long check our pursuers, but we had the satisfaction of learning that it threw them down an embankment, as will be narrated more fully in a Confederate account inserted hereafter.

When the engine first stopped, Andrews jumped off, clasped our hands in ecstasy, congratulating us that our difficulties were now all over; that we had the enemy at such a disadvantage that he could not harm us, and exhibited every sign of joy. Said he, "Only one more train to pass, and then we will put our engine to full speed, burn the bridges after us, dash through Chattanooga, and on to Mitchel at Huntsville." The programme would have been filled if we had met *only one* train.

We were ahead of time, and in order to meet the down train just *on* time, we were obliged to stop on the track awhile. These were tedious moments while we waited, but soon we moved on very slowly again. At the next station, Andrews borrowed a schedule from the tank-tender, telling him that he was running an express powder-train through to Beauregard. He gave the schedule, saying that he would send his shirt to Beauregard if he wanted it. When asked afterwards if he did not suspect anything, he said he would as soon have thought of suspecting Jeff Davis, as one who talked with so much assurance as Andrews did!

On we went till we reached the station where we were to pass what we believed to be the last train. Here the switch was not properly adjusted, and Andrews entered the station-house, without asking leave of anybody, took down the keys, and adjusted the switch. This raised some disturbance on the part of those around the station, but it was quieted by telling them the same powder story. After waiting a short time, the down train arrived, and we passed it without difficulty. But we observed on it what we did not like—*a red flag*, indicating that another train was behind.

This was most discouraging, for we had now hoped to have the road exclusively to ourselves; but still we did not despair. However, we had yet to run on regular time, which was, unfortunately, very *slow* time—not more than twelve or fifteen miles an hour. Thus unavoidably consuming our precious moments, we glided on till we reached the station where we expected to meet what we were now sure would be our last hindrance. We stopped on a side-track to wait for it, and there had to remain *twenty-five* minutes. Just as we had concluded to go on, and risk the chances of a collision, the expected train hove in sight.

It was safely passed, as the other had been before; but judge of our dismay when we beheld a *red flag* on this train also! Matters now began to look dark. Much of our precious time, which we had reserved as a margin for burning bridges, was now gone, and we were still tied down to the slow regular rate of running. Yet we could not retreat, and had no resource but to press firmly on. This we did, and obstructed the track as well as we could, by laying on cross-ties at different places. We also cut the telegraph wire between every station.

Finally, when we were nearly to the station where we expected to meet the last train, we stopped to take up a rail. We had no instruments for doing this, except a crowbar, and, instead of pulling out the spikes, as we could have done with the pinch burrs used for that purpose by railroad men, we had to *batter* them out. This was slow work. We had loosened this rail at one end, and eight of us took hold of it to try to pull the other end loose. Just as we were going to relinquish the effort in despair, the *whistle of an engine in pursuit sounded in our ears*! The effect was magical. With one convulsive effort we broke the rail in two, and tumbled pell-mell over the embankment. No one was hurt, and we took up our precious half rail, which insured us time to pass the train ahead, before our pursuers could be upon us.

We were not a moment too soon, for we were scarcely out of sight of where we had taken up the last rail, before the other train met us. This was safely passed, and when our pursuers came to the place where we had broken the rail, they abandoned their own train, and ran on foot till they met the one we had just passed, and turned it back after us, running with great speed.

We were now aware of our danger, and adopted every expedient we could think of to delay pursuit; but, as we were cutting the wire near Calhoun, they came in sight of us. Then ensued the most terrible and thrilling chase ever known on the American continent.

We instantly put our engine to full speed, and in a moment its wheels were striking fire from the rails in their rapid revolutions. The car in which we were, rocked furiously, and threw us from one side to the other like peas rattled in a gourd. Still on after us relentlessly came the pursuers. The smoke of their engine could be distinguished in every long reach, and the scream of their whistle sounded in our ears around every curve. It was still necessary for us to cut the wire, and, in order to gain time for that, we dropped a car on the track, and, soon after, another. This left us with only the locomotive, tender, and one baggage-car. Each time, when we stopped to cut the wire, we would try to take up another rail; but before we could loosen its fastenings with our imperfect tools, the approach of our enemies would compel us to hasten on.

The thought of a new expedient crossed my mind, which saved us for some time longer. It was to knock out the end of our car, and drop the rails on the track as we ran. Soon after, in one of our necessary stoppages to take care of the telegraph, we loaded on some cross ties, which we threw out in the same manner. One rail I reserved for a particular purpose. When we stopped again, I took it, placed one end under the track, and let the other project upward, jointing toward the advancing train. It was very nearly effectual. The engineer of the train in pursuit, who afterward visited us in prison, said that if it had been only one inch higher, nothing could have saved their train from wreck, because, being so dark and small, it was not noticed till too late to stop. However, it was a little too low to hook in the bars of the cow-catcher, as I intended.

Our enemies pursued us with great determination. One man rode on the cow-catcher, and, springing off, would throw the obstructions from the track, and jump on again while they had merely checked the engine. So great was our velocity, that most of the ties we threw out bounced off the track; but the few that remained enabled us several times to get out of sight of them. When this was the case, we would stop, and again try to take up a rail, which would have given us leisure for the greater operation of burning a bridge.

By this time we had a few more instruments, which Andrews and Wilson had simultaneously procured from a switch tender. We worked faithfully, but each time, before we had loosened a rail, the inexorable pursuers were again visible.

I then proposed to Andrews a plan that afforded a hope of final escape. It was to let our engineer take our engine on out of sight, while we hid on a curve after putting a tie on the track, and waited for the pursuing train to come up; then, when they checked to remove the obstruction, we could rush on them, shoot every person on the engine, reverse it, and let it drive at will back as it came. It would have chased all the trains following, of which there were now two or three, back before it, and thus have stopped the whole pursuit for a time. This would have required quick work, and have been somewhat dangerous, as the trains were now loaded with soldiers; but it afforded a *chance* of success. Andrews said it was a good plan—looked all around, and then hurried to the engine, and I had no further opportunity of discussing the subject. After we were in prison, he said he was very sorry that we had not made the effort.

Chapter 5
The Great Railroad Chase

All this time we were rushing through towns and villages at terrific speed. Some passengers came down when they heard our whistle, to go aboard, but they all shrank back amazed when they saw us pass with the noise of thunder, and the speed of lightning. Still more were they astonished when they saw three other trains dashing by in close pursuit, and loaded with excited soldiers. Thus the break-neck chase continued through Dalton, Ringgold, and the other small towns on the route.

But it soon became evident that it could not continue much longer. We had taken on wood and water before we were so closely pressed, but now our supply was nearly exhausted, and our pursuers were too close behind to permit us to replenish it. But before yielding, we resolved to try one more expedient.

For this purpose, we broke open the forward end of the only boxcar we had left, and with the fragments endeavoured to kindle a fire in it. Had we succeeded, we would have detached it, left it burning on a bridge, and run on with the locomotive alone. But the fuel on the latter was too nearly gone to afford us kindling wood, and the draught through the car, caused by our rapid motion, blew our matches out. At length we succeeded in kindling a small fire; but the drizzling rain, which had been falling all morning, blew in on it, and prevented it from burning rapidly enough to be of any service.

Thus our last hope expired, and our magnificent scheme, on which we had so long thought and toiled, was a failure. But one thing more now remained—to save ourselves, if possible.

We were within, perhaps, fifteen miles of Chattanooga, when we resolved to abandon the engine. Having made this resolve, we did not cut the telegraph wire, and then, for the first time, they succeeded in sending a message ahead of us.

This was no serious detriment to us, but it raised the wildest excitement in Chattanooga. The women and children instantly fled from the town, and sought safety in the woods and mountains. The whole military force, which was encamped near the place, came out, and selected an advantageous position to meet us. There they planted cannon, felled trees across the track, tore up the rails for some distance, and waited for our approach. Their orders were for them to make a general massacre—not to spare a single man. But we came not, and therefore they had no opportunity to display their latent cruelty.

It was at this point, when he saw every scheme we attempted to execute completely foiled, that Andrews' presence of mind, for a time, seemed to desert him. It was only fifteen miles across the country to the Tennessee river, and we could have reached it ahead of any opposition, had we all stuck together. One man had a compass, and with that, and Andrews' knowledge of the country, we could have gained, and crossed the Tennessee, and struck into the mountains beyond, before the country could have been aroused around us. Once there, in those interminable forests, it would have been almost impossible for them to capture us, well armed as we were, before we could have reached the shelter of our army. But this was not done, and this last chance of escape was lost.

The locomotive was run on till the wood and water were completely exhausted, and the pursuers plainly in view. Then Andrews gave the order for us to leave the train, disperse, and for every man to save himself, if he could. We obeyed, jumping off the train while still in motion, and were soon making the best of our way through the tangled pines of Georgia.

Before giving an account of our adventures in the woods, I will insert the following article from the *Southern Confederacy*, of April 15, 1862, a paper published in Atlanta, Georgia, only three days after our adventure. This I purloined from the officer in charge of us, and carried concealed about my clothes all the time I remained in the South. It contains a good many errors of statement, particularly where it refers to our numbers and plans, but is valuable as showing the estimate the rebels placed on our enterprise, and as giving their ideas of the chase. It also represents us as tearing up the railroad many more times than we did. In *no case* did they take up rails behind, and lay them down before their train. This assertion was made to give Messrs. Fuller and Murphy more credit at our expense. So highly were the services of these gentlemen appreciated, that the Georgia

State Legislature, in the fall of 1862, gave them a vote of thanks, and recommended the Governor to grant them the highest offices in his gift. I do not know what they actually did receive.

Below is the account:

THE GREAT RAILROAD CHASE!

The Most Extraordinary and Astounding Adventure of the War—The Most Daring Undertaking that Yankees ever Planned or Attempted to Execute—Stealing an Engine—Tearing up the Track—Pursued on Foot, on Hand-Cars, and Engines—Overtaken—A Scattering—The Capture—The Wonderful Energy of Messrs. Fuller, Murphy and Cain—Some Reflections, &c., &c.

FULL PARTICULARS!!

Since our last issue, we have obtained full particulars of the most thrilling railroad adventure that ever occurred on the American continent, as well as the mightiest and most important in its results, if successful, that has been conceived by the Lincoln Government since the commencement of this war. Nothing on so grand a scale has been attempted, and nothing within the range of possibility could be conceived, that would fall with such a tremendous, crushing force upon us, as the accomplishment of the plans which were concocted and dependent on the execution of the one whose history we now proceed to narrate.

Its *reality—what was actually done—*excels all the extravagant *conceptions* of the Arrow-Smith hoax, which fiction created such a profound sensation in Europe.

To make the matter more complete and intelligible, we will take our readers over the same history of the case which we related in our last, the main features of which are correct, but are lacking in details, which have since come to hand.

We will begin at the breakfast-table of the Big Shanty Hotel at Camp McDonald, on the Western and Atlantic Railroad, where several regiments of soldiers are now encamped. The morning mail and passenger train had left here at four A. M., on last Saturday morning, as usual, and had stopped there for breakfast. The conductor, William A. Fuller; the engineer, I. Cain, both of this city; and the passengers were at the table, when some eight men, having uncoupled the engine and three empty box-cars next to it, from the passenger and baggage-cars, mounted the engine, pulled open the valve, put on all steam, and left conductor, engineer, passengers, spectators, and the soldiers in the camp hard by, all lost in amazement, and dumbfounded at the strange, startling, and daring act.

This unheard-of act was, doubtless, undertaken at that place and time upon the presumption that pursuit could not be made by an engine short of Kingston, some thirty miles above, or from this place; and that by cutting down the telegraph wires as they proceeded, the adventurers could calculate on at least three or four hours' start of any pursuit it was reasonable to expect. This was a legitimate conclusion, and but for the will, energy, and quick good judgment of Mr. Fuller, and Mr. Cain, and Mr. Anthony Murphy, the intelligent and practical foreman of the wood department of the State Road shop, who accidentally went on the train from this place that morning, their calculations would have worked out as originally contemplated, and the results would have been obtained long ere this reaches the eye of our readers—the most terrible to us of any that we can conceive as possible, and unequalled by any attempted or conceived since this war commenced.

Now for the chase!

These three determined men, without a moment's delay, put out after the flying train—*on foot*, amidst shouts of laughter by the crowd, who, though lost in amazement at the unexpected and daring act, could not repress their risibility at seeing three men start after a train on foot, which they had just witnessed depart at lightning speed. They put on all their speed, and ran along the track for three miles, when they came across some track-raisers, who had a small truck-car, which is shoved along by men so employed on railroads, on which to carry their tools. This truck and men were at once "impressed." They took it by turns of two at a time to run behind this truck, and push it along all up grades and level portions of the road, and let it drive at will on all the down grades. A little way further up the fugitive adventurers had stopped, cut the telegraph wires, and torn up the track. Here the pursuers were thrown off pell mell, truck and men, upon the side of the road. Fortunately "nobody was hurt on our side." The truck was soon placed on the road again; enough hands were left to repair the track, and with all the power of determined will and muscle, they pushed on to Etowah Station, some twenty miles above.

Here, most fortunately, Major Cooper's old coal engine, the *Yonah*—one of the first engines on the State road—was standing out, fired up. This venerable locomotive was immediately turned upon her own track, and like an old racer, at the tap of the drum, pricked up her ears and made fine time to Kingston.

The fugitives, not expecting such early pursuit, quietly took in wood and water at Cass Station, and borrowed a schedule from the tank-tender, upon the plausible plea that they were running a pressed train, loaded with powder, for Beauregard. The attentive and patriotic tank-tender, Mr. William Russell, said he gave them his schedule, and would have sent the shirt off his back to Beauregard, if it had been asked for. Here the adventurous fugitives inquired which end of the switch they should go in on at Kingston. When they arrived at Kingston, they stopped, went to the agent there, told the powder story, readily got the switch-key, went on the upper turn-out, and waited for the *down way freight train to pass*. To all inquiries they replied with the same powder story. When the freight train had passed, they immediately proceeded on to the next station—Adairsville—where they were to meet the regular *down freight train*. At some point on the way they had taken on some fifty cross-ties, and before reaching Adairsville, they stopped on a curve, tore up the rails, and put seven cross-ties on the track—no doubt intending to wreck this down freight train, which would be along in a few minutes. They had out upon the engine a red handkerchief, as a kind of flag or signal, which, in railroading, means another train is behind—thereby indicating to all that the regular passenger train would be along presently. They stopped a moment at Adairsville, and said Fuller, with the regular passenger train, was behind, and would wait at Kingston for the freight train, and told the conductor thereon to push ahead and meet him at that point. They passed on to Calhoun, where they met the down passenger train, due here at 4.20 P. M., and without making any stop, they proceeded—on, on, and on.

But we must return to Fuller and his party, whom we have unconsciously left on the old *Yonah*, making their way to Kingston.

Arriving there, and learning the adventurers were but twenty minutes ahead, they left the *Yonah* to blow off, while they mounted the engine of the Rome Branch Road, which was ready fired up, and waiting for the arrival of the passenger train nearly due, when it would have proceeded to Rome. A large party of gentlemen volunteered for the chase, some at Acworth, Altoona, Kingston, and other points, taking such arms as they could lay their hands on at the moment; and with this fresh engine they set out with all speed, but with great "care and caution," as they had scarcely time to make Adairsville, before the down freight train would leave that point. Sure enough, they discovered, this side of Adairsville, three rails torn up and other impediments in the way. They "took up" in time to prevent an accident, but could proceed with the train no further. This was most vexatious, and it may have been in some degree disheartening; but it did not cause the slightest relaxation of efforts, and, as the result proved, was but little in the way of the *dead game*, pluck and resolutions of Fuller and Murphy, who left the engine and again *put out on foot alone!* After running two miles, they met the down freight train, one mile out from Adairsville. They immediately reversed the train, and ran backwards to Adairsville—put the cars on the siding, and pressed forward, making fine time to Calhoun, where they met the regular down passenger train. Here they halted a moment, took on board a telegraph operator, and a number of men who again volunteered, taking their guns along—and continued the chase. Mr. Fuller also took on here a company of track-hands to repair the track as they went along. A short distance above Calhoun, they *flushed their game* on a curve, where they doubtless supposed themselves out of danger, and were quietly oiling the engine, taking up the track, &c. Discovering that they were pursued, they mounted and sped away, throwing out upon the track as they went along, the heavy cross-ties they had prepared themselves with. This was done by breaking out the end of the hindmost box-car, and pitching them out. Thus, "nip and tuck," they passed with fearful speed Resaca, Tilton, and on through Dalton.

The rails which they had taken up last they took off with them—besides throwing out cross-ties upon the track occasionally—hoping thereby the more surely to impede the pursuit; but all this was like tow to the touch of fire to the now thoroughly-aroused, excited, and eager pursuers. These men, though so much excited, and influenced by so much determination, still retained their well-known caution, were looking out for this danger, and discovered it, and though it was seemingly an insuperable obstacle to their making any headway in pursuit, was quickly overcome by the genius of Fuller and

Murphy. Coming to where the rails were torn up, they stopped, tore up rails behind them, and laid them down before, till they had passed over that obstacle. When the cross-ties were reached, they hauled to and threw them off, and thus proceeded, and under these difficulties gained on the frightened fugitives. At Dalton they halted a moment. Fuller put off the telegraph operator, with instructions to telegraph to Chattanooga to have them stopped, in case he should fail to overhaul them.

Fuller pressed on in hot chase—sometimes in sight—as much to prevent their cutting the wires before the message could be sent, as to catch them. The daring adventurers stopped just opposite and very near to where Colonel Glenn's regiment is encamped, and cut the wires; but the operator at Dalton *had put the message through about two minutes before*. They also again tore up the track, cut down a telegraph pole, and placed the two ends of it under the cross-ties, and the middle over the rail on the track. The pursuers stopped again, and got over this impediment in the same manner they did before—taking up the rails behind, and laying them down before. Once over this, they shot on, and passed through the great tunnel at Tunnel Hill, being there only five minutes behind. The fugitives, thus finding themselves closely pursued, uncoupled two of the box-cars from the engine, to impede the progress of the pursuers. Fuller hastily coupled them to the front of his engine, and pushed them ahead of him, to the first turn-out or siding, where they were left, thus preventing the collision the adventurers intended.

Thus the engine-thieves passed Ringgold, where they began to fag. They were out of wood, water, and oil. Their rapid running and inattention to the engine had melted all the brass from the journals. They had no time to repair or refit, for an iron-horse of more bottom was close behind. Fuller and Murphy, and their men, soon came within four hundred yards of them, when the fugitives jumped from the engine, and left it, three on the north side, and five on the south side; all fleeing precipitately, and scattering through the thicket. Fuller and his party also took to the woods after them.

Some gentleman, also well armed, took the engine and some cars of the down passenger train at Calhoun, and followed up Fuller and Murphy and their party in the chase, but a short distance behind, and reached the place of the stampede but a very few moments after the first pursuers did. A large number of men were soon mounted, armed, and scouring the country in search of them. Fortunately, there was a militia muster at Ringgold. A great many countrymen were in town. Hearing of the chase, they put out on foot and on horseback in every direction, in search of the daring, but now thoroughly frightened and fugitive men.

We learn that Fuller, soon after leaving his engine, in passing a cabin in the country, found a mule, having on a bridle but no saddle, and tied to a fence. "Here's your mule," he shouted, as he leaped upon his back, and put out as fast as a good switch, well applied, could impart vigour to the muscles and accelerate the speed of the patient donkey. The cry of "Here's your mule," and "Where's my mule," have become national, and are generally heard when, on the one hand, no mule is about, and on the other when no one is hunting a mule. It seems not to be understood by any one, though it is a peculiar Confederate phrase, and is as popular as Dixie, from the Potomac to the Rio Grande. It remained for Fuller, in the midst of this exciting chase, to solve the mysterious meaning of this national by-word or phrase, and give it a practical application.

All of the eight men were captured, and are now safely lodged in jail. The particulars of their capture we have not received. This we hope to obtain in time for a postscript to this, or for our second edition. They confessed that they belonged to Lincoln's army, and had been sent down from Shelbyville to burn the bridges between here and Chattanooga; and that the whole party consisted of nineteen men, eleven of whom were dropped at several points on the road as they came down, to assist in the burning of the bridges as they went back.

When the morning freight train which left this city reached Big Shanty, Lieutenant-Colonels R. F. Maddox and C. P. Phillips took the engine and a few cars, with fifty picked men, well armed, and followed on as rapidly as possible. They passed over all difficulties, and got as far as Calhoun, where they learned the fugitives had taken the woods, and were pursued by plenty of men, with the means to catch them if it were possible.

One gentleman who went upon the train from Calhoun, who has furnished us with many of these particulars, and who, by the way, is one of the most experienced railroad men in

Georgia, says too much praise cannot be bestowed on Fuller and Murphy, who showed a cool judgment and forethought in this extraordinary affair, unsurpassed by anything he ever knew in a railroad emergency. This gentleman, we learn from another, offered, on his own account, one hundred dollars reward on each man, for the apprehension of the villains.

We do not know what Governor Brown will do in this case, or what is his custom in such matters; but if such a thing is admissible, we insist upon Fuller and Murphy being promoted to the highest honours on the road; if not by actually giving them the highest position, at least let them be promoted by *brevet*. Certainly their indomitable energy, and quick, correct judgment and decision in the many difficult contingencies connected with this unheard-of emergency, has saved all the railroad bridges above Ringgold from being burned; the most daring scheme that this revolution has developed has been thwarted, and the tremendous results which, if successful, can scarcely be imagined, much less described, have been averted. Had they succeeded in burning the bridges, the enemy at Huntsville would have occupied Chattanooga before Sunday night. Yesterday they would have been in Knoxville, and thus had possession of all East Tennessee. Our forces at Knoxville, Greenville, and Cumberland Gap, would, ere this, have been in the hands of the enemy. Lynchburg, Virginia, would have been moved upon at once. This would have given them possession of the Valley of Virginia, and Stonewall Jackson could have been attacked in the rear. They would have possession of the railroad leading to Charlottesville and Orange Court House, as well as the South Side Railroad leading to Petersburg and Richmond. They might have been able to unite with McClellan's forces, and attack Jo. Johnston's army, front and flank. It is not by any means improbable that our army in Virginia would have been defeated, captured, or driven out of the State this week.

Then reinforcements from all the Eastern and Southeast portion of the country would have been cut off from Beauregard. The enemy have Huntsville now, and with all these designs accomplished, his army would have been effectually flanked. The mind and heart shrink appalled at the awful consequences that would have followed the success of this one act. When Fuller, Murphy, and Cain started from Big Shanty *on foot, to capture that fugitive engine*, they were involuntarily laughed at by the crowd, serious as the matter was—and to most observers it was indeed most ludicrous; but *that footrace saved us*, and prevented the consummation of these tremendous consequences.

One fact we must not omit to mention, is the valuable assistance rendered by Peter Bracken, the engineer on the down freight train which Fuller and Murphy turned back. He ran his engine fifty and a half miles—two of them backing the whole freight train up to Adairsville—made twelve stops, coupled to the two cars which the fugitives had dropped, and switched them off on sidings—all this, *in one hour and five minutes.*

We doubt if the victory of Manassas or Corinth were worth as much to us as the frustration of this grand *coup d' etat.* It is not by any means certain that the annihilation of Beauregard's whole army at Corinth would be so fatal a blow to us as would have been the burning of the bridges at that time and by these men.

When we learned by a private telegraph dispatch, a few days ago, that the Yankees had taken Huntsville, we attached no great importance to it. We regarded it merely as a dashing foray of a small party to destroy property, tear up the road, &c., *a la* Morgan. When an additional telegram announced the Federal force there to be from 17,000 to 20,000, we were inclined to doubt—though coming from a perfectly honourable and upright gentleman, who would not be apt to seize upon a wild report to send here to his friends. The coming to that point with a large force, where they would be flanked on either side by our army, we regarded as a most stupid and unmilitary act. We now understand it all. They were to move upon Chattanooga and Knoxville as soon as the bridges were burnt, and press on into Virginia as far as possible, and take all our forces in that State in the rear. It was all the deepest laid scheme, and on the grandest scale, that ever emanated from the brains of any number of Yankees combined. It was one that was also entirely practicable on almost any day for the last year. There were but two miscalculations in the whole programme; they did not expect men to start out afoot to pursue them, and they did not expect these pursuers on foot to find Major Cooper's old *Yonah* standing there all ready fired up. Their calculations on every other point were dead certainties, and would have succeeded perfectly.

This would have eclipsed anything Captain Morgan ever attempted. To think of a parcel of Federal soldiers, officers and privates, coming down into the heart of the Confederate States—for they were here in Atlanta and at Marietta—(some of them got on the train at Marietta that morning, and others were at Big Shanty;) of playing such a serious game on the State Road, which is under the control of our prompt, energetic and sagacious Governor, known as such all over America; to seize the passenger train on his road, right at Camp McDonald, where he has a number of Georgia regiments encamped, and run off with it; to burn the bridges on the same road, and to go safely through to the Federal lines—all this would have been a feather in the cap of the man or men who executed it.

Let this be a warning to the railroad men and everybody else in the Confederate States. Let an engine never be left alone a moment. Let additional guards be placed at our bridges. This is a matter we specially urged in the Confederacy long ago. We hope it will now be heeded. Further, let a sufficient guard be placed to watch the government stores in this city; and let increased vigilance and watchfulness be put forth by the watchmen. We know one solitary man who is guarding a house in this city, which contains a lot of bacon. Two or three men could throttle and gag him, and set fire to the house at any time; and worse, he conceives that there is no necessity for a guard, as he is sometimes seen off duty for a few moments, fully long enough for an incendiary to burn the house he watches. Let Mr. Shakelford, whom we know to be watchful and attentive to his duties, take the responsibility at once of placing a well-armed guard of sufficient force around every house containing government stores. Let this be done without waiting for instructions from Richmond.

One other thought. The press is requested by the Government to keep silent about the movements of the army, and a great many things of the greatest interest to our people. It has, in the main, patriotically complied. We have complied in most cases, but our judgment was against it all the while. The plea is that the enemy will get the news if it is published in our papers. Now, we again ask, what's the use? The enemy get what information they want. They are with us and pass among us almost daily. They find out from us what they want to know, by passing through our country unimpeded. It is nonsense—it is folly, to deprive our own people of knowledge they are entitled to and ought to know, for fear the enemy will find it out. We ought to have a regular system of passports over all our roads, and refuse to let any man pass who could not give a good account of himself, come well vouched for, and make it fully appear that he is not an enemy, and that he is on legitimate business. This would keep information from the enemy far more effectually than any reticence of the press, which ought to lay before our people the full facts in everything of a public nature.

CHAPTER 6

The Greatest Manhunt in the South

On leaving the train, I confess for a moment my heart sunk within me. I was alone, for no one happened to strike off in the same direction I did. I knew not where I was—whether fifteen or fifty miles from Chattanooga[2]—neither had I the most indefinite idea of the lay of the country. I only knew that north or northwest would bring me to our forces; but the sun did not shine, to give me even the points of the compass.

I supposed that the country would be aroused, and a vigorous pursuit made, but my worst anticipations proved far short of the reality. It was Saturday, the 12th of April, and was a general muster-day for the conscripts over the whole country; but as soon as the news of our raid was received, drill was suspended, and every one turned out in search of us. Then was organized the most stupendous *man-hunt* that ever took place in the South. Horsemen hurried at full speed along every road, and proclaimed the news as they went. Each planter, with his dependents, for at least fifty miles in every direction, took his bloodhounds and scoured the woods. Every cross-road, every river, ford, or ferry, was at once picketed by bodies of cavalry. Large rewards were offered, and thousands of soldiers pursued us, in addition to the universal uprising of the citizens. The only partially known object of the expedition imparted a tone of romantic exaggeration to it, and made the people doubly anxious to solve the mystery. The feeling in northern Georgia may be best conceived by imagining what would be the excitement in the immediate vicinity, if a party of Confederates would seize a train near Philadelphia, and attempt to run it through Baltimore, especially if the movements of their armies should be such as would lead to the belief that this was only *part* of a grand scheme!

---

2. The description of places and distances given in the preceding chapter, was mostly obtained from Confederates, who afterward visited and talked with us.

I will now give a personal sketch of my own adventures after leaving the train. It was still moving when I jumped off,—fast enough to make me perform several inconvenient gyrations on reaching the ground. Most of the party were ahead of me. Three had taken the eastern side of the road, and the remainder the opposite side. I followed the example of the latter, and soon reached the cover of the stunted pines that grew near the road. Feeling the necessity of getting away as far as possible before the enemy could pursue us on foot, I struck off at a rapid rate.

Soon I passed the little brook that ran along the foot of the hill, and pressed on up its steep side. There were three of my comrades not far from me on the left, but I could not overtake them, and still proceeded alone. I knew that pursuit would be rapid and instantaneous. I seemed to hear the tread of cavalry in every breeze that sighed through the branches of the naked forest!

The country was rough and uneven. On the bottoms, and by the streams, were a few pines; but on the mountain spurs, which here are a low continuation of the Cumberland range, the timber is mostly oak and other varieties, which were not then in foliage. This was a great disadvantage, because it left no hiding place, and exposed us to the view of the watchful eyes of our enemies.

Soon I found myself in the bend of a little river that empties into the Tennessee at Chattanooga. It was swollen by continuous rains, and for some time I searched along its bank for a place to cross the turbulent stream; but, seeing none, and believing that death was behind, I committed myself to its angry current, and, after being thoroughly soaked, and almost washed away, I succeeded in reaching the opposite side. Here the bank rose in an almost perpendicular precipice of more than a hundred feet in hight. I dared not recross the stream, for I knew the enemy could not be far behind, and, therefore, I clambered up the precipice. Several times when near the top did I feel my grasp giving way; but as often did some bush or projecting rock afford me the means of saving myself. At last, after the most imminent danger, I reached the top utterly exhausted, pulled myself out of sight, and breathed for a while.

I had had no breakfast or dinner, and had spent not only that day, but many preceding ones, in the most fatiguing exertion. I was very faint and sick, and almost out of hope. I had no guide even in the direction of home, for the sun still lingered behind an impenetrable veil.

While I thus lay and mused on the unenviable situation in which I found myself placed, a sound reached my ears that again sent the blood leaping wildly through my veins. It was the distant baying of a bloodhound! Never again will I read the story of human beings, of any color, pursued by these revolting instruments of man's most savage "inhumanity to man," with indifference!

I started to my feet, and a few moments' listening confirmed my first impression. It was true. They were after us with their bloodhounds! not one pack alone, but all in the country, as the widening circle, from which echoed their dismal baying, revealed but too plainly. There was no longer safety in idleness, and I at once started up, and hurried off, as nearly at right angles to the railroad as I could ascertain by the whistling of the trains, which seemed to be moving in great numbers, and much excited. The fearful barking of the dogs also gave me a clue to avoid them. Faint and weak as I was, excitement supplied the place of strength, and I rapidly placed a considerable distance between myself and pursuers.

Away across the hills and streams I sped, I knew not how far—I only knew that the noise of the dogs grew fainter and fainter as the evening wore on. I had distanced them, and began to breathe freer. I even indulged the hope of being able ultimately to work my way to the lines, and still think I might have done so, had the weather been clear enough to permit my traveling by the sun or stars.

As I descended the long slope of a wooded hill into a wild, solitary valley, I saw a rude hut, and a man in the garden beside it. I approached him to inquire the road to Chattanooga, though that was the last place I wished to go. The answer was, that it was only eight miles. This was nearer than I liked to be, as I rightly judged the pursuit would be most vigorous in that vicinity. However, I continued my journey in that direction, until out of sight, and then climbed up the hill at right angles to my former course. I traveled this way for some time, when an incident occurred that would have been amusing, had it been less vexatious.

I had often heard that persons who were lost would naturally travel in a circle, but did not attach a great deal of credit to the assertion. Now I had the proof. I had crossed a road, and left it for something like an hour, during which time I walked very fast, when, to my surprise, I came to the same place again.

I was considerably annoyed to thus lose my labour, but struck over the hill in what I supposed to be the right direction. Judge of my astonishment when, after an hour or more of hard walking, I found myself at precisely the same spot again! So much time had been lost, that I now could hear the bloodhounds once more. I was perplexed beyond measure. A few steps further brought me to the *same river* I had crossed hours before. In sheer desperation I took the first road I came to, and followed it a long time, almost regardless of where it should lead, or whom I should meet.

Thus I pressed forward till twilight was deepening into darkness, when I met a negro driving a team. From him I learned that I was within four miles of Chattanooga; words can not describe the tide of vexation, disappointment, and anger that swept over my breast, when I found that in spite of my most determined efforts I was steadily approaching the lion's mouth. But it was no use to give way to despair. Learning from the negro the direction of both Ringgold and Chattanooga, I resolved to make an effort to reach the Tennessee river some eight or ten miles below Chattanooga. For this purpose, I struck across the fields in the proper course.

For some time now I did well enough, but before long I came to a large field of deadened timber. When I had crossed this, I was again completely lost. Soon, however, I reached a road which seemed to lead right, which I followed with renewed vigor for several miles. At last I met three men on horseback; it was too dark to tell whether they were negroes or white men, but I ventured to ask them:

"How far is it to Chattanooga?"

"*Three miles!*"

"Is this the road?"

"Yes, sah! *Right ahead.*"

I had afterwards reason to believe that these were men sent out to arrest us, and that they did not stop me just because I was going right to Chattanooga!

But it was evident that I was again on the wrong road. Indeed, it seemed as if I was so hopelessly bewildered that it was impossible for me to travel any *but* the wrong road. As soon as the horsemen got out of sight, I turned and followed them three or four miles, when I came to a large road running at right angles with my own, which terminated where it joined the other. I deliberated for some time as to which end of this new road I should take. I had no guide to direct me, for my old road was too crooked even to give me the direction of the dreaded Chattanooga.

Many a time have I wished for a sight of the moon and stars. Long before the clash of arms was heard in our land, before the thunder and the wailing of battle had filled a nation with weeping, have I waited and wished for the parting away of the tedious clouds, that, with my telescope, I might gaze on the wonders and beauties of the worlds above. But never did I bend a more anxious eye to the darkened firmament, than in my solitary wanderings over the Georgia hills that memorable night. But all in vain; no North Star appeared to point with beam of hope to the land of the free.

At length I started off on the road that I thought most likely to lead me in the right direction; but as usual I had the misfortune of being wrong; for after I had gone a long distance, the moon broke through a rift in the clouds, and for a moment poured her light down on the dark forest through which I was passing. That one glance was enough to show me that I was heading back toward the railroad I had left in the morning. Wearily I turned and retraced my tedious steps.

One of my feet had been injured by an accident three mouths before, and now pained me excessively. Still I dragged myself along. My nerves had become completely exhausted by the long-continued tension they had sustained, and now played me many fantastic tricks, which became more vivid as the night waned away. I passed the place where I had made the wrong choice of roads, and still toiled on.

The rain fell in torrents now. I was thinly clad, and as the wind, which was blowing quite hard, drove the falling showers against me, my teeth chattered, and I shivered to the bone. I passed many houses, and feared the barking of the dogs might betray me to watchers within; but my fears were groundless. The storm, which was then howling fearfully through the trees, served to keep most of those who sought our lives, within doors. Even the barking of the bloodhounds was heard but seldom, and then far in the distance. I seemed to have the lonely, fearful, stormy night to myself.

At last all thoughts gave way to the imperative necessity of repose. I reeled to a large log that lay by the side of the road, on the edge of a small patch of woodland, and crawling close under the side of it, not for shelter from the driving rain, but for concealment from my worse-dreaded human foes, I slept in peace.

Up to this time the image of that terrible night is graven on my memory with a scorching pen of fire. After this it changes, and with the exception of a few real incidents that aroused me from my trance, it floats before me in more than the voluptuous splendor of an opium-dream. The cause of this change is a curious chapter in mental philosophy. It was no doubt purely physical, resulting from want of sleep, fatigue, dampness, lack of food, and intense mental exertion. But let me narrate facts.

When I awoke, it was with a full realization of my position. But in addition to this, I seemed to hear some one whisper, as plainly as ever I heard human voice:

"Shoot him! Shoot him! Let us shoot him before he wakes!"

My first impression was, that a party of rebels had discovered my hiding-place, and were about to murder me in my sleep, to save themselves further trouble. But the next thought brought a new suspicion, and I cautiously opened my eyes to test it, and see if my senses were really playing false.

Directly before me stood a small tree. The first glance showed a tree and nothing more. The next showed a score of angels, all clad in softest outlines, their heads nodding with feathery plumes above all beauty, and their wings slowly waving with borders of violet and pearl. The whole forest was suddenly transformed into a paradise of radiant glory, in which moved celestial beings of every order, all instinct with life, blushing with love, and bending their kindest regards on me. Ladies, too, were there, fairer than ever walked the fields of earth, embowered in roses; little cherubs with laughing faces, on cloudlets of amber and gold, floated around. Indeed, all that the imagination could conceive of beauty was comprised in that one gorgeous, glorious vision.

The most singular fact of all was, that although the brain and eye were thus impressed with that which had no real existence, I was perfectly calm and self-possessed, knowing the whole thing to be but a pleasing illusion. I did not in the least fear these figures of the brain, but on the contrary found them pleasant company. Not always, however, did they personate the same characters. Occasionally they would change to the old feudal knights, sometimes on horseback, sometimes on foot, but always clad in glittering armor.

The finest landscapes would start up from the cold, dull hills around, like mirages in the desert; panoramas of the most vivid action passed before me; even language was not denied to my visitants, whose voices were inexpressibly melodious; every thought that passed through my mind seemed sounded audibly at my side.

Thus through the visions of night and darkness I passed rapidly on, for now I felt refreshed and endowed with new strength. Even the merciless pelting of the cold rain seemed pleasant and luxurious as a cool bath in the parching heats of harvest. But beyond these illusions, another faculty seemed to penetrate and show me, though but dimly, the true face of the country.

Once the two became mingled, and very nearly involved me in a serious difficulty. At a cross-road, a considerable distance ahead, I saw what I at first supposed to be some more of my spectral friends, standing around a fire, the ruddy blaze of which served to render them clearly visible. They were not quite so beautiful as those I had seen before, but still I advanced carelessly toward them, and would probably have continued to do so, until too late for retreat, had not my progress been arrested by a sound of all others the least romantic. It was the squealing of a pig they had caught, and were killing, preparatory to roasting in the fire.

This at once drove away the seraphs and the angels, and left me in full possession of my faculties. I listened, and soon became convinced that they were a picket, sent out there to watch for just such persons as myself. They had some dogs with them, which, fortunately, were too much absorbed in the dying agonies of the poor pig to give attention to me.

I crawled cautiously away, and made a long circuit through the fields. A dog made himself exceedingly annoying by following and barking after me. I did not apprehend danger from him, for I yet had my trusty revolver, and had managed to keep it dry all the time; but I feared he would attract the attention of the picket, who might easily have captured me, for I was too weary to elude them.

At last he left me, and I again returned to the road. I had not gone far till I came to three horses hobbled down, which, no doubt, belonged to the picket behind, and had to make another circuit to avoid driving them away before me. On again reaching the road, I pressed on as fast as possible, hoping, before the morning light, to be beyond the circle of guarded roads, and the line of planters who were scouring the woods with their dogs. It was a vain hope, but I knew not then the gigantic plan of search which had been organized.

The visions which had made the lonely forest almost a paradise, now grew dimmer and dimmer. The roses faded, and all the forms of beauty vanished into thin air.

The chill horror of my situation froze deeper into my veins. I would find myself walking along, almost asleep, then would wander a short distance from the road to a secluded spot,—throw myself down on the flooded ground, and sleep a few minutes; then would awaken, almost drowned by the pitiless rain, and so sore and benumbed that I could scarcely stagger to my feet, and plod onward.

Thus that dreary night wore on; it seemed an age of horror, and placed a shuddering gulf between my present life and the past. But at last the cold gray of a clouded morning broke through the weeping sky. Day brought no relief. Every one I saw seemed to be a foe. Still I did not avoid them. I carefully washed all traces of that terrible night from my clothes. The wet did not matter, for the rain was still falling fast enough to account for that.

Chapter 7

All Abandon Hope

It was Sabbath morning, but it came not to me with the blessed calmness and peace that accompany it in my own sweet Ohio. I saw the people going to church, and longed to go with them, but dared not encounter the prying eyes that would have greeted a stranger, even if I had wished thus to loiter on my journey.

But why should I dwell longer on this dreary morning? why linger over its miseries, deepened by the faintness of the hope that they would ever cease, and give me again to the comfort and love of home? I wandered on till about noon, when I was observed by some one on the watch for strangers. This was just beyond Lafayette, Georgia. A party of pursuit was at once organized numbering twenty or more. I knew nothing of my danger, till they were within about fifty yards of me, when they ordered me to stop.

I put my hand on my pistol, and looked round. The country was level and open for some distance, and I was too weary to run, even if some of the party had not been mounted; therefore I made a virtue of necessity, and stopped, asking what they wanted. They replied that they wanted to talk with me awhile. Soon they came up, and a little, conceited man, who had the epaulets of a lieutenant, but whom they called major, undertook to question me. He was very bland about it, and apologized hugely for interrupting me, but said if I was a patriotic man, as he had no doubt I was, I would willingly undergo a slight inconvenience for the good of the Confederacy. I endeavored to imitate his politeness, and begged him to proceed in the performance of his duty, assuring him that he would find nothing wrong. He then searched me very closely for papers, looking over my money and pistol, but found nothing suspicious.

He next asked me who I was, where I came from, and where I was going. I told him that I was a citizen of Kentucky, who had been disgusted with the tyranny of Lincoln, and was ready to fight against it; that I came to Chattanooga, but would not enlist at that place, because most of the troops there were conscripts, and the few volunteers were very poorly armed. I told him all about where I had been in Chattanooga, and the troops there, for I had heard a good deal said about them as I went down on the cars to Marietta, on the previous Friday evening. I had also heard them praising the First Georgia, which was with Beauregard, and now told the Major that I wanted to join it. He then asked why I did not proceed at once to Corinth, without going so far around the country. I alleged that General Mitchel was in the way at Huntsville, and that I was merely making a circuit far enough around to be out of the danger of capture.

This seemed to be perfectly satisfactory to the little man, and turning to the crowd he said:

"We may as well let this fellow go on, for he seems to be all right."

These words rejoiced me, but my joy was premature. A dark-complexioned man, who sat on his horse, with his hat drawn down over his brows, raised his eyes slowly, and drawled out:

"Well, y-e-s! Perhaps we'd as well take him back to town, and if all's right, maybe we can help him on to Corinth."

This was rather more help than I wanted, but it was useless to demur.

They conducted me to the largest hotel in the place, where I was received very kindly. Soon a number of lawyers came in, and commenced asking me all kinds of hard questions. I answered as well as I could. When I told them I was from Kentucky, they wished to know the county. I told them Fleming. Then they asked the county seat. This also I was able to give; but when they required me to give the counties which bounded it, I was nonplussed. I mentioned a few at random, but suspect most of them were wrong. They said it looked suspicious to find a man who could not bound his own county, but proceeded in their examination.

They requested a narrative of my journey all the way through from Kentucky. This I gave very easily, as long as it was on ground that was not accessible to them; but it sorely puzzled me to account for the time I had been on the railroad, and for the last night, which I spent in the woods. I had to *invent* families with whom I stayed—tell the number of children and servants at each, and all the particulars. This was rather perilous, as many of my auditors knew all the country around which I was thus fancifully populating; but I had no alternative. I might have refused to answer at all, but this would have been construed into positive proof of guilt—at least as good as a *mob* would have required. Besides, I still had a faint hope that they might be induced to release me, and allow me to continue my journey. As it was, my assurance puzzled them somewhat, and they held numerous private consultations.

But while they were thus deliberating over my case, and could only agree that it needed further investigation, a man, riding a horse covered with foam, dashed up to the door. He came from Ringgold, and brought the news that part of the bridge-burners had been captured, and that they had at first pretended to be *citizens of Kentucky, from Fleming county,*—but, on finding that this did not procure their release, they confessed that they were Ohio soldiers, sent out to burn the bridges on the Georgia State Road.

The remarkable coincidence of their first story with the one I had been trying so hard to make the rebels believe, produced a marked change in their conduct toward me. They at once adjourned to another room, and, after a brief consultation, agreed to commit me to jail to await further developments.

The little major was my escort. He first purloined my money, then took me to the county jail and handed me over to the jailor. This personage took my penknife and other little articles,—then led me up stairs,—unfastened the door of a cage of crossing iron bars, in which was one poor fellow—a Union man, as I afterward found—and bade me enter. My reflections could not have been more gloomy if the celebrated inscription, Dante, placed over the gates of hell, had been written above the massive iron door.

"All hope abandon, ye who enter here."

My feelings were terrible when the jailor turned the key in the lock, secured the heavy iron bar that crossed the door, and left me. Never before had I been locked up as a prisoner, and now it was no trivial matter—a few days or weeks. There was absolutely no hope ahead. I was there as a criminal, and too well did I realize the character of the Southern people, to believe that they would be fastidious about proof. Life is held too cheap in that country to cause them a long delay in its disposal.

In that hour, my most distressing thought was of my friends at home, and particularly of my mother—thinking what would be their sorrow when they heard of my ignominious fate—if indeed they ever heard, for I had given an assumed name. That all my young hopes and ambitions, my fond dreams of being useful, should perish, as I then had no doubt they would, on a Southern scaffold, seemed unbearable in the extreme. But only one moment did these thoughts sweep over me; the next they were rejected as not calculated to profit in the least. My first action was to borrow from my Union companion his blankets, of which he had a plentiful supply, and wrap myself in them. The warmth they produced soon threw me into a deep sleep,—profound and dreamless,—such as only extreme fatigue can afford.

I awoke hours after, feeling much refreshed, but did not at first realize where I was; yet a glance at the woven bars which everywhere bounded me in, brought back the knowledge that I was a prisoner; but I did not give way to useless despair. I was almost amused at the quaint, yet truthful remark my fellow-prisoner made to me. Said he:

"If you are innocent of the charge they have against you, there is no hope for you. But if it is true, you may save yourself by telling what regiment and company you belong to, and claiming protection as a United States prisoner of war."

I thought a good deal over this opinion, and became more and more impressed with its wisdom. It contained a truth that I could not gainsay. To hang a poor stranger in the South would be a commonplace affair—only what was often done by the Southerners before the war began. In fact, they did kill a man at Dalton, under circumstances of the greatest cruelty, because he cheered as we dashed through the town. Afterward they found out that the man was as good a rebel as any of them, and had merely cheered because he thought we, too, were rebels; then they set the matter right by apologizing to his friends!

It was quite different in the case of our soldiers. If they were murdered, there was an unpleasant probability that some of the chivalry themselves would have to suffer in retaliation. Besides, I reflected with a glow of hope, the first I experienced since I fell into their hands, that our government held a number of rebels, who had been taken in Missouri on a similar expedition. All day and night I mused on these things, and endeavored to come to such a decision as would be for the best. When I heard of the capture of many of our party, and the announcement of the regiments to which they belonged, showing that they had been influenced by the same considerations I had been revolving, I at once determined to rest my fate on my claim as a United States soldier. I believe that this decision ultimately saved my life.

All this time I was not in loneliness. Throngs of Georgians came in to see the caged Yankee—both ladies and gentlemen. Many were the odd remarks they made, criticising every feature, and not a few adding every possible word of insult. The whole day they crowded in, and I was glad when the approach of night put an end to the annoyance.

The coarse food the jailor brought was eaten with such a relish as hunger only can impart. I was fortunate in respect to quantity, for my companion was not well, and could not eat much; but I atoned for his shortcoming by eating both of our allowances without difficulty.

In the morning, they took me before a self-constituted committee of vigilance. These committees were very common in the South, and still more summary in their modes of administering justice, or rather vengeance, than were the celebrated vigilance committees of San Francisco, in the early history of the gold mines. They were prepared with a board of the most eminent lawyers in the vicinity, and no doubt hoped to entangle me still more deeply in the meshes of contradiction than they did the day before. But I cut the whole matter short by saying:

"Gentlemen, the statements I gave you yesterday were intended to deceive you. I will now tell you the truth."

The clerk got his pen ready to take down the information.

"Go on, sir; go on," said the president.

"I am ready," said I, "to give you my true name and regiment, and to tell you why I came into your country."

"Just what we want, sir. Go on," said they.

"But," I returned, "I will make no statement whatever, until taken before the regular military authority of this department."

This took them by surprise, and they used every threat and argument in their power to induce me to change my purpose, but in vain. My reason for this, was to avoid the violence of mob law. While in the hands of the populace, there was danger of the summary infliction of punishment that the military authorities could disavow, if our government threatened retaliation. But if I was once under the regular military jurisdiction, they would be responsible both to the United States and to the civilized world.

When they found that I would tell them nothing further, they made arrangements to take me to Chattanooga, which was distant twenty miles. It was the same to Ringgold, near which we abandoned the train. Thus it will be seen that in that long and terrible night I had traveled twenty miles in a straight line, and, with my meanderings, must have walked fifty.

I was remanded to the jail to wait for the preparation of a suitable escort. Here I remained till after dinner, when I was guarded by about a dozen men to the public square. A carriage was in waiting, in which I was placed, and then commenced the process of tying and chaining.

A great mob gathered around, completely filling the whole square, and was exceedingly angry and excited. They questioned me in loud and imperious tones, demanding why I came down there to fight them, and adding every possible word of insult. I heard many significant hints about getting ropes, and the folly of taking me down to Chattanooga, when I could be hanged just as well there.

However, as the mob grew more violent in their denunciations, I selected some of the more intelligent ones and addressed them. They answered with curses; but in the very act of cursing, they grew milder and more willing to converse. I was not very much in the humor for talking, but following the dictates of policy rather than inclination, I answered their innuendoes merrily, and soon had some of the laughers on my side. Before long, I heard some of them say, "Pity he is a Yankee, for he seems to be a good fellow." This was gratifying, and we were soon ready to start.

I had been secured in such a manner as to make assurance doubly sure. A heavy chain was put around my neck and fastened by a padlock; the other end was hitched to one foot, and secured in the same manner; the chain being extended to its full length, while I was in a sitting position, making it impossible for me to rise.—My hands were tied together; my elbows were pinioned to my side by ropes; and, to crown all, I was firmly bound to the carriage seat!

My evil genius, the little major, took the seat beside me as driver. He was armed to the teeth. Two other officers on horseback, likewise fully armed, constituted the rest of the guard that was thought necessary to attend one chained and helpless Yankee. Oh! spirit of chivalry! how art thou fallen! No longer one brave Southern knight a match for eight or ten Northern mudsills; but three well-armed officers to guard one chained Union soldier! The same exaggerated caution I frequently noticed afterward. There seemed to be a perpetual fear on the minds of the miscreants that we were about to do something desperate.

As we journeyed along, the sky, which for days had been overcast, and, during that time, had hardly afforded us a glimpse of its celestial blue, became suddenly clear. The sun shone out in beauty, and smiled on the first faint dawnings of spring that lay in tender green on the surrounding hills. I am ever very sensitive to the influences of nature in all its phases, and now felt my spirit grow more light as I breathed the fresh air, and listened to the singing of the birds.

My companions were quite talkative, and though I hated them for the indignity they had thus put upon me in chaining me as a criminal, yet I knew it would be unavailing to indulge a surly and vindictive disposition, and therefore talked as fast and as lively as they could.

My guards, themselves, did not subject me to any insults, and even endeavored to prove that the extraordinary manner in which I was bound was a compliment to me. I could not see it in that light, and would have willingly excused the tying and the compliment together! The worst was that when they passed any house they would call out, "We've got a live Yankee here;" then men, women, and children, would rush to the door, and stare as though they saw some great monster, asking:

"Whar did you ketch him? Goin' to hang him when you get him to Chattanooga?" and similar expressions without end.

This was only amusing at first, but its perpetual recurrence soon grew terribly wearisome, and was not without its effect in making me believe they really would hang me. In fact, my expectation of escaping was never very bright; yet I considered it my duty to keep up my spirits as well as I could, and not despair till it really was certain that there remained no ground for hope. The afternoon wore slowly away as we traveled along, passing some very grand and romantic scenery, that in any other frame of mind would have been enthusiastically enjoyed; but now my thoughts were otherwise engaged.

It was not the thought of death I so much dreaded, as the manner of death. Death amid the smoke, and excitement, and glory of battle, was not half so terrible as in the awful calmness and chill horror of the scaffold! And sadder yet, to think of my friends, who would count the weary months that had gone by, and wish and long for my return, till hope became torturing suspense, and suspense deepened into despair. These thoughts were almost too much for stoicism; yet there was no alternative but to patiently endure.

The sun went down, and night came on—deep, calm, and clear. One by one the stars twinkled into light. I gazed upon their beauty with new feelings, as I wondered whether the short, revolving course of a few more suns might not bring me a dweller above the stars! And as I thought of the blessed rest for the weary beyond the shores of time, my thoughts took a new direction. I was not then a professor of Christianity, but had often and believingly thought of the great interests of the future, and had resolved to make them my particular study; but had never hitherto addressed myself in earnest to the task, and latterly, the confusion and bustle of a camp-life had almost driven the subject out of my mind. But now, whether it came from the clustering stars above, or from the quiet and stillness so congenial to exhausted nature, after the weariness and excitement of the last few days, or from a still deeper source, I know not. I only know that the memory of that night, when I was thus being carried chained to an unknown fate, is one of the sweetest of my life. My babbling guards had subsided into silence, and, as we wended along through the gathering darkness, high and noble thoughts of the destiny of man filled my breast, and death seemed only the shining gate to eternal and blissful life. I was nerved for any fate.

We arrived at Chattanooga while a feeble glow of the soft spring twilight still lingered on the earth. We immediately drove to the headquarters of General Leadbetter, then commanding that place, and while our guards ascended to inform him of our arrival, I was left in the carriage. As soon as we entered the town, the word was given:

"We've got a live Yankee; one that took the train the other day."

I was not the first one of the party captured, but was the first brought to Chattanooga. The curiosity to see one of the men who had frightened women and children into the woods, was, of course, most extreme, and an immense crowd soon gathered around. They behaved just as Southern mobs usually do—jeering and hooting—calling me by every epithet of reproach the language afforded, and wanting to know why I came down there to burn their property, and murder them and their children. To these multitudinous questions and assertions I made no answer. I was greatly amused—afterward!—by their criticisms on my appearance. One would say that "it was a pity that so young and clever-looking a man should be caught in such a scrape." Another, of more penetrating cast, could tell that "he was a rogue by his appearance—probably came out of prison in his own country." Another was surprised that I could hold up my head and look around on honest men—arguing that such brazen effrontery was a proof of enormous depravity of heart. I did not give my opinion on the subject. Indeed, it was not asked.

There was one man I noticed in particular. He was tall and venerable-looking; had gray hair, gray beard, a magnificent forehead, and an altogether commanding and intellectual expression of countenance. He was treated with great deference, and appeared to me most like a doctor of divinity. As he parted his way through the crowd toward me, I thought:

"Surely I will receive some sympathy from that noble-looking man."

His first question was calculated to confirm my impression. Said he: "How old are you?"

I answered, "Twenty-two, sir."

Gradually his lip wreathed itself into a curl of unutterable scorn, as he slowly continued:

"Poor young fool! and I suppose you was a school-teacher, or something of that kind in your own land! and you thought you would come down here and rob us, and burn our houses, and murder us, did you? Now let me give you a little advice: if you ever get home again, (but you never will,) do try, for God's sake, and have a little better sense, and stay there!"

Then he turned contemptuously on his heel, and strode away, while the rabble around rewarded him with a cheer. I never could find out who he was. After that I looked no more for sympathy in that crowd.

My conductors now returned, and escorted me into the presence of General Leadbetter. They said he was a Northern man; but if so, it is very little credit to my section, for he was one of the most contemptible individuals I ever knew. He was a perfect sot, and had just two states of body, as a Confederate captain afterwards explained to us—these were, dead drunk, and gentlemanly drunk. He oscillated constantly between these two. He was a coward as well, and though only a brigadier-general, managed to stay as far away from the field when the fight was going on, as one of our own most conspicuous major-generals did. He had been promoted to his present position for his *gallantry* in hanging some defenceless East Tennessee citizens, which he did without a trial.

All these facts I learned afterward, except one, which was apparent when I entered the room. He was "gentlemanly drunk." He commenced questioning me, and I told him partly the truth, and partly not—going on the principle that truth is a pearl, and pearls are not to be thrown before swine. I told him that I was a United States soldier, giving him my company and regiment; but saying that I was detailed without my consent, that I was ignorant of where I was going, and what I was to perform, which I only learned as fast as I was to execute it. He wanted to know our intention in thus seizing the engine, but I plead ignorance. He next inquired who was our engineer, but I refused to tell. He then said:

"Sir, I want you to tell me just how many men you had on that train, and to describe them so I may know when I get them."

I answered, "General, I have freely told you whatever concerns only myself, because I thought it better that you should know that I am a soldier under the protection of the United States, but I have not yet become base enough to describe my comrades!"

"O!" sneered he, "I don't know that I ought to have asked you that."

"I think not, sir," I replied.

"Well," said he, "I know all about it. Your leader's name is Andrews. What kind of a man is he?"

I was perfectly astonished that he should have Andrews' name, and know him to be our leader; but I never imagined what I afterward found to be the true cause—that Andrews had been captured, and had given his name, with the fact that he was the leader of the expedition. I had every confidence that *he* would get away, and try some measures for our relief; so I answered boldly:

"I can tell you only one thing about him, and that is, he is a man whom you will never catch."

I *thought* I noticed a peculiar smile on the General's face as I said this, but he only replied:

"That will do for you;" and turning to a captain who stood by, he continued, "take him to the hole; you know where that is."

With a nod in reply, the captain took me out of the room. As I passed through the door, I saw an explanation of the General's smile. There stood Andrews, ironed, waiting an audience, and Marion Ross and John Williams with him. I did not choose to recognize them; for such recognition might have compromised them, as I knew not what course they would pursue.

Chapter 8

Cast Into Cimmerian Gloom

The captain now called a guard of eight men, and conducted me through the streets for some time; at last we came to a little brick building, surrounded by a high board fence. Those who have ever been in Chattanooga, and visited the negro prison, will recognize my description. A portion of the building was occupied by the jailor, but the prison part consisted of two rooms, one under the other, and also partly underground. This under room had no entrance from the outside, but was accessible only through a trap-door from the room directly overhead.

Chattanooga is not a county-seat, and, therefore, this prison was built only for the accommodation of negroes by their humane owners.

The jailor, Swims, was a character, and merits a particular description. He was an old man—perhaps sixty. His hair, which was very abundant, was white as snow, and his face had a dry and withered expression. His voice was always keyed on a whining tone, except when some great cause, such as the demand of prisoners for an extra bucket of water, excited him, and then it rose to a hoarse scream. Avarice was his predominant, almost his only, characteristic. He seemed to think his accommodations were vastly too good for negroes and Yankees, and that when they were admitted within his precincts, they should be thankful, and give as little trouble as possible. With such notions, it was not wonderful that he managed to make the lot of the prisoner an uncomfortable one. In addition to this, he was very fond of a dram, and frequently became sufficiently intoxicated to reveal many important matters that we would not otherwise have learned.

He bustled to the gate, growling all the time about being troubled so much, unlocked it, and admitting us, led us up the outside stairway, and then into the upper room. I now saw why the General called the place a "hole," and truly I thought the name was appropriate. It was only thirteen feet square, destitute of every convenience, without chairs, beds, or anything of the kind. There were in it five or six old, miserable-looking men, who had not been washed for months. The place looked hard to me, and I shuddered at the idea of taking up my abode in such a den. But I soon found that I was not to enjoy that luxury.

Said the jailor to the captain, "Where shall I put him?"

"Below, of course," was the reply.

The jailor then advanced to the middle of the floor, and taking a large key from his pocket, knelt down and unlocked two rusty locks; then, with a great effort, raised a ponderous trap-door just at my feet. The hot air and the stifling stench smote me back, but the bayonets of the guards were just behind, and I was compelled to move forward again. A long ladder was next thrust down through the trap-door, and the inmates warned to stand from under. A mingled volley of cries, oaths, and questions ascended, and the ladder was secured. The captain then ordered me to descend into what seemed more like Pandemonium than any place on earth. Down I went into the *cimmerian* gloom—clambering step by step to a depth of fully thirteen feet; for the place, as I afterwards learned, when I had more leisure for observation, was a cube, just thirteen feet each way. I stepped off the ladder, treading on human beings I could not discern, and crowding in as best I might.

The heat was so great that the perspiration broke from me in streams. The foeted air made me for a time deadly sick, and I wondered whether it could be possible they would leave human beings in this horrible place to perish. The thought of the black hole at Calcutta, where so many Englishmen died, rushed over me. True, this was done by the cruel and savage East Indians, while we were in the hands of "our Southern brethren," the "chivalry;" but I could not perceive that this difference of captors made any difference of treatment.

My breath came thick and heavy, and I thought of suffocation. The ladder was drawn up, and with a dull and heavy sound that seemed crushing down on my heart, the trap-door fell. I wedged and jammed my way through the living throng to the window. The one I reached was just under the wooden stairs, and, of course, gave no light. The other was below the surface of the ground. They were at opposite sides of the room, and were only about a foot square, being filled with a triple row of thick set iron bars, that almost excluded every current of air. I pressed my face close to the bars, and breathed the purest air I could get, until I became partly reconciled to the oppression, and then turned to ascertain the condition of my companions. It was wretched beyond description. They were ragged, dirty, and crawling with vermin. Most of them were nearly naked; but this was no inconvenience there, for it was so warm that those who had clothes were obliged to take them off, and nearly all were in a state of nudity. I soon found it necessary myself to disrobe, and even then the perspiration poured off me most profusely. It was an atmosphere of death.

Yet among the prisoners were old men, just trembling on the verge of the grave, who were arrested merely because they had ventured to express a preference for the old, well-tried Government, over the new, slave-built Confederacy. The cruelty practiced on the Tennessee Union men will never half be told. It forms the darkest page in the history of the war. In every prison of which I was an inmate in Georgia and Virginia, as well as in Tennessee, I found these miserable but patriotic men thus heartlessly immured. But I will speak more of them hereafter; at that time the thought of my own danger banished every other consideration.

There were fourteen white men in the room beside myself, and one negro. I wonder what those tender soldiers, who consider it derogatory to their dignity to fight in the same army that blacks do, would think if they were confined with them so closely that there was no possibility of getting away. But we endured too many real evils to fret at imaginary ones; and besides, Aleck was so kind and accommodating, so anxious to do everything in his power for us, that he soon became a general favorite; and when he was taken out to be whipped, as he was several times, to ascertain whether he was telling a true story or not, we could not help feeling the sincerest sympathy for him.

The Southern method of catching stray negroes is about this: When one is found traveling without a pass, he is arrested, taken to the jail, and severely flogged. This usually brings some kind of a confession from him, and he is advertised in accordance with that confession. If no answer is received in a limited time, it is taken for granted that he lied, and he is whipped again, in order to bring a new confession. Thus they continue alternately whipping and advertising, till the close of the year. If a master is found before this, he can pay the costs and take his property; if not, the negro is sold to pay the jail and whipping fees. No trial is ever allowed at which the negro might prove himself free. When once arrested his doom is sealed, and in this way many free negroes are enslaved.

Aleck had been in this prison seven months, and was to remain five more, with no other prospect than that of being sold into perpetual bondage!

Every society has its aristocrats, and here I soon found that the eminence was given to those who were charged with the most daring deeds. The spy—there was but one so accused, and he was blind,[3]—was considered much above the ordinary Union men. I was charged with the greatest adventure of any confined there, and, of course, was treated with becoming deference.

I was not long the only one of the *engine-thieves*—by which name we were known during our stay in the Confederacy—who was confined in this dungeon. Soon the trap-door again opened, causing a stream of comparatively cool air from the room above to rush down. It was an inconceivable relief—a *luxury* that none could appreciate who had not, as we had, been deprived of that greatest blessing God has given to man—pure air.

We wondered who was coming next, as the feeble glimmering of a candle above revealed several forms descending. The Tennesseeans cried out:

"Don't put any more down here! We're full! We'll die if more are put down!" which did not seem improbable.

But these remonstrances produced no effect. Down they came, and I, stationing myself at the foot of the ladder, spoke something indifferently to them, and heard my name called in return.

It was Andrews, Wollam, and Ross, who gave me their hands in silent condolence of our common misery. Still others were brought, I do not now remember whether that evening, or in the morning. Again the door was closed, and the free air, which had seemed to flow to us in sympathy, was once more shut out.

We tried to arrange ourselves to secure the repose we so much needed, but the room was too small. Think of this, ye who sleep on your downy beds at home. Here were your brothers of Ohio, not only compelled to sleep on the bare floor, but not even enough of that, in this vilest of dens, on which to lie down at all! and yet some of you sympathize with those who were the authors of this cruelty, and think it so hard that their property should be confiscated for such trifles as these, and, worst of all, that their negroes should be taken from them! What shall we think of *you*?

We did the best we could. Some found room to lie down. Others sat against the wall, and still others leaned on the breasts of those who were thus supported. It is no wonder if, while in such a situation we should be afflicted with the nightmare, and have innumerable bad dreams. If

---

3. The rebels thought he was counterfeiting blindness, but I believe it was real.

any one wanted to move his position, or go for a drink, (and the stifling heat rendered us all very thirsty,) he was sure to tread on his neighbors, and tempers being naturally very short here, some warm altercations took place, which contributed still more to disturb our slumbers.

The next morning we slept late. Indeed, as long as we remained in this prison we were inclined to sleep much. The great quantity of carbonic acid gas our breathing produced, seemed to act as an opiate, and thus served, in some measure, to deaden the sense of pain. We were aroused the next morning—early, as we supposed—by the opening of the door above, and the delicious shower of cool air that fell on us. As we looked up, we saw the white head of our old jailor bending over, and saying, in drawling tones, "Boys, here's your breakfast," and down he lowered a bucket, by a rope, containing a very small piece of bread, and the same of meat, for each of us. This was seized and devoured almost instantly. I had received nothing to eat since breakfast the day before, and the little morsel I got only served to whet my appetite; but there was no more! We asked what time it was, and were told nine o'clock. We were also informed that we would get our meals only twice a day. This was rather discouraging information for persons as hungry as ourselves, but we had no remedy.

During the day a few more of our party came in, and among them was G. D. Wilson. I found that they had all done as I had in acknowledging themselves United States soldiers, influenced by the same reasons, and most of them sooner than myself. We consulted about the matter, and concluded that the only hope we had, was in adhering to the same story, and trying to make them believe that we were actually detailed without our consent, and without a knowledge of what we had to do. This was true for part, but not for all, or even for the most of us. We agreed to conceal the name of the engineer at all hazards—the fact of a previous expedition being sent down into Georgia, and that Campbell was not a soldier—also our previous acquaintance with Andrews, thus leaving him free to make his own defense. With the exception of these reserved facts, which were not even to be whispered among ourselves, we were to talk freely; to answer all questions and convey the impression that we had nothing to conceal. We carried out this idea, and, as more of our men came in, they agreed to it, and gave, without reserve, their true names, companies, and regiments. This course gained us sympathy from those whose bosoms were not steeled against every kindly feeling; and to this, more than anything else, I attribute the fact of some of the party being alive to-day.

We afterward communicated our plan to Andrews, who cordially approved it—saying that if we adhered to it there would be some chance for our lives. We did adhere to it, and no amount of persuasion, threatening, or promises, could induce any of the party to betray one of our reserved secrets. The rebels were particularly anxious to discover who was the engineer, and would first ask the question in the most careless manner; then afterward would sternly demand to know. They even employed a man, who was a freemason, to visit the party, and try to gain the confidence of one of our number, who belonged to that order, and subsequently urge him to tell the desired name, under the sanction of the masonic oath! But all in vain.

As others of our party joined us, in bands of two or three, they told the story of their capture. This was, in some cases, most thrilling, and still further illustrates the fiendish barbarities of the rebels.

Two of them, Parrott and Robinson, who were captured the same day they left the train, were taken to Ringgold. Here they endeavored to compel Parrott, who was the youngest looking of the party, to betray his companions, and particularly the engineer; but he refused to do it; then these villains in Confederate uniform, stripped him naked, and stretched him down on a rock, four men holding him by each hand and foot, while two others stood by with loaded revolvers, threatening him with instant death if he offered the least resistance; then a rebel lieutenant commenced whipping him with a raw hide; three different times he ceased and raised Parrott up, asking him if he was ready to confess; but the heroic boy refused, and at last the whipping was discontinued, after more than a hundred lashes had been inflicted. His back remained sore a long time, and he suffered very much from being obliged to lie on the hard floor. They did not apply anything to his wounds to heal them, and the scars still remain.

All the party came in chained, but of course expected, when they were put down into the dungeon—and *such* a dungeon!—that they would at least have the use of their hands. But this was too great an indulgence to be allowed. We were handcuffed, and then chained together by the neck in twos and threes. My partner was William Reddick, to whom I was *strongly attached* for some time!

Thus chained together, packed into a little cramped dungeon, deprived even of light, and almost of air, crawled over by all kinds of vermin, for there were innumerable rats, mice, and bugs, as well as a smaller and still more pestiferous insect, we presented a picture of nearly perfect misery.

In this state we remained almost three weeks. During this time Andrews had received a trial. The evidence was strong against him. A Mr.

Whiteman, whom Andrews himself had directed to be summoned, and who was a former business partner of his, testified that Andrews had been repeatedly in the South, that he had professed allegiance to the Southern Confederacy, and in all things represented himself to be a citizen of the same. In fact he had passes in his possession when he was captured that could hardly have been obtained without his taking the oath of allegiance. This did much to sustain the charge of treason against him, as he admitted being the leader of the expedition. The other indictment, which was that of being a spy, was not supported by any evidence, so far as I could learn; but this was of no importance, as the punishment of the first charge was death. However, the sentence was not then given, and Andrews' lawyers gave him some reason to hope that there was an informality in the proceedings which would render the whole trial void.

All this time we were most intensely anxious to know how military affairs were progressing in the world without. I had appropriated from an officer in charge of us, a paper containing the Confederate account of our chase, which has been given before, and also an admission that the battle of Shiloh was not so much of a victory as they had at first supposed. We managed, likewise, to get one or two other papers which gave the welcome news that our armies were still pressing onward, and earnestly did we wish and hope that Chattanooga would be reached in time to effect our deliverance.

But the best item of news we received, was from our old jailor, who, on one occasion, became too drunk to remember the orders he had received against telling us anything, and let out the very interesting fact that General Mitchel had advanced to Bridgeport, only twenty-eight miles below us, on the Tennessee river, and there had sorely defeated the rebels, capturing some of the very same men who had been guarding us a few days before.

This was very cheering, and we began to hope that we, too, would soon be captured. The officer of the guard was obviously uneasy. All the time we were in the dungeon, we had been guarded by twenty-six men, with a captain over them. This was certainly enough to keep twenty-two, confined and chained as we were, in our place, but we thought it would be a capital joke should they be captured with us!

But it was not their intention to let us fall into Mitchel's hands. An order was sent to the captain in charge to prepare us for moving. He did so; and soon after, we were in the cars, carried down the same road we came up so rapidly three weeks before.

How beautiful all nature appeared! It was May, and the time we had spent without one glance at the expansive sky or green earth, had not been lost in the material world. The landscape had been robed in a richer verdure, the budding trees had swelled into leafy screens, the sky was of a softer blue, the birds warbled with new melody, and everything seemed to wear its holiday dress.

O, the joy! the gladness! of being once more under the canopy of heaven, and of looking up to its unfathomable depths, with no envious bars to obstruct our view. Many a time have I passed the month of May, amidst the most romantic scenery, but never yet did I so deeply feel, that this is indeed a pleasant world, full of beauty and goodness, as on that balmy evening, when the rays of the setting sun, glowing from the west, streamed over the grass and wheatfields on their path, and poured in mellowed, yellow radiance, through our car-window. But even then the glories of earth and sky could not make me forget that I was still chained to my companion, and surrounded by guards with gleaming bayonets.

The wild excitement caused by our raid had not subsided in the least, and as it became known that we were passing along the road, a mob greeted us at every station. It is not necessary to again describe these mobs, for all are alike, and one description answers for many. They were, as usual, rude, loquacious, and insulting.

When we arrived in Atlanta, which was in the morning, there was no jail-room for us; but before going further, we were obliged to wait for the evening train. When it became known in the city that we were there, a mob instantly collected, and prepared to hang us. They were prevented by our guard, probably on the principle that a mouse is protected by a kitten—that it may have the pleasure of first playing with it, and afterwards killing it itself. During the progress of the strife between those who wanted to hang us and those who wanted the law to take its course, several persons were severely injured. But while the disturbance was in progress, one man succeeded in reaching the car window unnoticed, and handed us a paper, using only the single but magical word—"a friend"—and then was lost in the throng. We read the paper by snatches as the attention of the guard was directed to other objects, and found it to contain glorious news—nothing less than *the capture of New Orleans by our fleet!* Need I say that, for the time, all thought of private misfortune was lost in the exhilaration of national triumph?

The cause of secession then looked gloomy. I took particular pains to talk with the officer in charge of us, and other intelligent rebels, about their prospects, and found them discouraged. Our captain would not let us have any newspapers, or *knowingly* give us any information; yet he thought it no harm to talk with us on the great subject of the war, after we had learned the facts from other sources. Frequently, by pretending to know, we could get from him a full idea of things concerning which we were ignorant before. Of this character was McClellan's advance on Richmond. The captain admitted that he was moving with an overwhelming force, and that they had then but a comparatively small army to resist him. Indeed, everything looked bright for the Union cause, and the only uneasiness that disturbed us was the apprehension that we might not live to witness that happy triumph which now seemed so near.

In the evening we glided on again, and at length arrived at Madison. This is a flourishing village, and looked well as we entered it. There were then some six hundred of our prisoners confined there, and we indulged the hope that we might be put with them. But we soon learned that the brand of criminality for our daring adventure still rested on us; for we were marched past the dilapidated cotton factory where our friends were confined, to the old county jail, which was then entirely unoccupied. It was a gloomy stone building, and had two rooms, but both had doors, and were above ground. Of the upper story I can not speak, as our party was divided, and I was one that was assigned to the lower apartment. The room was very dark, and its heavy stone walls rendered it quite damp. It would have seemed like a wretched place, had it not been for our previous experience in Chattanooga. Besides, we were now further from the influence of General Leadbetter, and only under the control of our captain, who showed us some kindness, though we were still in irons.

The citizens of the place were freely admitted to see us, and ranged themselves—always in the presence of the guard—along one side of the cell, and talked about all the exciting topics of the day. They pretended to admire us very much, and contrasted our daring expedition with what they were pleased to call the cowardice of the Yankees generally, and asked if there were any more like us in the army. Wilson, of Cincinnati, assured them that we were the poorest men in Mitchel's Division, and only sent away because he had no use for us. This rather astonished them; but from the way in which Mitchel, with his small and divided force, was controlling Northern Alabama, and much of Eastern Tennessee, as well as defeating them at all points, they were rather inclined to believe it.

But among these visitors was one who came not for mere curiosity. He was dressed in rebel uniform, but was instantly recognized by

Andrews as *a spy in the service of the United States*. They had no opportunity for private communication, but our situation was revealed in such a way as not to excite suspicion. His character was made known to us by Andrews, after his departure; and while we were wondering at his audacity, and rather inclined to disbelieve the story, the captain of the guard, who had come to bring supper, told us that a most remarkable occurrence had taken place that afternoon.

He said that the Provost-Marshal had learned, from some source, that a spy of Lincoln's had been among our visitors, and had at once sent a guard to arrest him. The guard found him at the depot, just as the cars were coming in. The stranger was very indignant at his arrest, and told them scornfully that he had papers in his pocket that would prove his character anywhere. They were somewhat abashed at this, and released their hold on him, but asked him to produce the papers. He put his hand in his pocket, as though searching for them, and fumbled about, until he noticed that the train, which was starting, had attained a good rate of speed, and then, just as the last car swung by, he dashed from them, and jumped aboard! There was no telegraph station at Madison, and he escaped.

At this the Confederates were very much enraged, and would permit no more visiting; but we felt ample consolation in the certainty that our condition would be at once reported to our officers, and every effort made for our release.

Chapter 9
Imprisonment & Escapes

We remained only three days in Madison, when the rebel general, becoming convinced that Mitchel was not then going to advance on Chattanooga, ordered us back to that place. Again we were compelled to run the gauntlet of insulting and jeering mobs that had annoyed our course down the road. We traveled in rude box-cars, that were wet and filthy, and the journey was rendered still more uncomfortable by the idea of going back to our old quarters in the wretched prison at Chattanooga.

However, by the time we arrived there, our captain, who had never been a very warm secessionist, and, therefore, had no very hard feelings towards us, had become quite friendly. He now proved this by interceding in our behalf, and procuring us permission to remain in the upper room. This was the same size as the lower one, but it had three windows instead of two, and these were larger, and obscured by only one row of bars. But the poor Tennessee Union men had to go below.

It was amusing to see the exaggerated caution with which they guarded us. Even when we were below, where scarcely any man could have got out without assistance, they never raised the trap-door unprotected by a strong guard. Now, when we were in the upper room, their vigilance was still further increased. They would bring a guard into the jailor's room, through which ours was entered, and there array them with leveled bayonets, into two lines across the door. At the same time, the stairway was guarded, and another guard always surrounded the jail outside of the wall. And even the old jailor would fret, and predict that evil would result from showing the Yankees so much indulgence.

All this time we were chained, and as the authorities were thus slow in relieving us of what we believed to be an unnecessary incumbrance, we set our wits to work to free ourselves. One of the party had managed to secrete a small knife while they were searching him, and with this made rude keys from the bones of the meat given us, and in a short time opened every lock. We could not, of course, appear in public in our new liberty, or more effectual means of fastening would probably have been devised. To avoid detection, we kept some one always on the watch. Then, when any person was heard approaching our room, a signal was given, and a quick rattling of chains accompanied the adjustment and re-locking of our bands. When the door opened, we would be chained all right, and as soon as it closed we would be free again. We continued this deception during our stay in this prison, and were never detected.

While here, we relieved the tedious time that hung heavily on our hands by mock trials. We would charge one of the company with some offence, generally a trifling breach of our prison rules, and proceed to trial. Campbell, whose immense personal strength better enabled him to inflict the punishment that would be awarded, usually officiated as judge, until at last he got the name of Judge firmly fixed on him. These trials produced much sport. We had ample time for it, and the opposing counsel would make very long and learned speeches. So interesting were these arguments, and so eloquent our appeals, that no one of the auditors was ever known to leave the house while they were in progress! The witnesses, too, were very slippery, and it was sometimes quite difficult to reconcile their testimony. There were always some nullifiers present who would attempt to resist the enforcement of the laws, and the infliction of the penalties adjudged; but in these cases the *personal weight* of the judge decided the matter. This resistance would give rise to new arrests and trials, and thus the work became interminable.

Another and more refined enjoyment was singing. There were several good singers in the party, and, by practicing together, they soon acquired great proficiency. Most of the songs were of a tender and melancholy cast; such as the "Carrier Dove," "Do They Miss Me at Home," "Nettie More," "Twenty Years Ago," &c. Our time for singing was when twilight began to fall. Then in the gathering darkness the voice of song would ring out, as glad and free as if it was not strained through prison bars. The guards liked very much to hear us sing, and frequently citizens of the town would gather round outside to listen to the caged Yankees.

There is one man in the Confederacy whom I must praise. Amid the worthless and boastful aristocrats who have monopolized for themselves the name of "chivalry," I found *one* gentleman. This was Colonel Claiborne, at that time Provost-Marshal of Chattanooga. When he first visited us, he said boldly that it was a shame to keep men in such a condition, and tried in vain to get permission from General Leadbetter, to remove our irons; he then ordered us to be brought into the yard to breathe the fresh air every afternoon. This was an inexpressible relief, for it was now intensely hot in our room; and simply to be in the open air a short time was a luxury above all price. This he did on his own responsibility, and some weeks afterward was dismissed from his post on account of his humanity to us!

While here, the idea of escape frequently presented itself. It is true that our guards outnumbered us, and always used the cautions I have described above; but the very fear this argued would have been our best help. We often discussed the subject among ourselves.

All were anxious to go but Ross and Wilson, who thought the proposition premature, as they, relying on what the officers in charge of us said, believed that there was some hope of our exchange. But others of us were impatient to make one bold effort for our own deliverance. Two plans were proposed. The first, which I suggested, was to have all our irons off when the guards came up to feed us, and then, as the door opened, to make a simultaneous rush on the leveled bayonets outside, wrest the arms from their owners, and pour down stairs on the guard below. As soon as we had secured the arms of the remainder, we could leave the prison-yard in a solid body, and pass on double-quick to the ferry-boat, which lay on our side of the river, not far distant. Once over the river, and thus armed, we would have been comparatively safe.

The other plan, which we finally agreed to adopt, was proposed by Andrews. It was, that some one should secrete himself under the bed in the jailor's room, when we were coming up from our breathing in the yard, and remain there till all was quiet at night; then come out and noiselessly unlock the door; after this, we could rush down, seize the guard, and proceed, as in the first plan.

There were two of our party who failed to reach the place of rendezvous in time to be with us on the train. One was from the Twenty-first, the other from the Second Ohio Regiment. They were suspected, and to save themselves, were compelled to join a rebel battery, which they did, representing themselves as brothers from Kentucky. In the battle at Bridgeport, in which the secessionists were so badly panic-stricken, the one from the Twenty-first found an opportunity to escape to General Mitchel. This caused suspicion to rest on his supposed brother, who was arrested, brought to Chattanooga, and confined in the dungeon while we were there. We recognized him, and talked, though very cautiously, about his adventures. He asked us not to divulge the fact that he was one of us—an unnecessary request. He remained there for some time, and was finally released, and put into the battery again, from which, by a wonderful series of adventures, he succeeded in making good his escape to our lines.

At this time there was a great talk of exchange. A son of General Mitchel's had been captured; but he also held a considerable number of prisoners, and it was believed that an exchange would be effected. A lieutenant, whom Mitchel had released on parole, for the purpose of seeing Kirby Smith, at that time commanding the department of East Tennessee, and obtaining his consent to an exchange, visited us. His story raised the most sanguine hopes. The Confederate officers, however, said that it would be first necessary to have a trial, and prove that we were really United States soldiers, and then we, too, would be embraced in the exchange. Andrews, some time before, wanted to send a flag of truce through the lines to get from our officers a statement of our true character; but they refused permission, saying that they could believe our own story on the subject without going to so much trouble.

The prospect of an exchange served to defer our attempted escape, but at last we resolved to wait no longer. The very day we came to this conclusion, an order was given to send twelve to Knoxville for trial—a mere formal one as the commander of the guard and the marshal told us—to clearly prove that we were an authorized military expedition, and not mere citizen adventurers. George D. Wilson was in the yard when the order came. He was permitted to be down there, because he was very sick. The officer of the guard handed him the order, asking him to select twelve to go, as no names were mentioned. He did so, selecting all his own regiment (Second Ohio) first, and afterward his special friends from the other regiments, because he thought it would be a favor to them—that they would probably be first exchanged. This unexpected order induced us to abandon our cherished scheme of escape, which, in all probability, judging from the result of a subsequent attempt, under far more unfavorable circumstances, would have been completely successful.

As we twelve, who were to go to Knoxville, prepared for our departure, we felt a shade of gloom fall over our spirits. Our little band, who had for nearly two months been companions in dangers and privations, such as few men ever experienced, was now to be divided, and we knew not where we should unite again; for in spite of their fair words, the *fact* remained that we were in the power of that enemy who has deluged our land in blood.

With Andrews, the parting was peculiarly affecting; we had been accustomed to look up to him in all emergencies. He was our leader, and was the particular mark for the vengeance of the foe. Officers, in bidding us hope, spoke no words of comfort to him. He bore this like a hero, as he was, and continued to hope against hope. But *now*, after we had sung our songs together for the last time, and come to bid him farewell, we were moved even to tears. I will never forget his last words, as he silently pressed our hands, and with a tear in his blue eye, and a low, sweet voice, that thrilled through my inmost being, said: "Boys, if I never see you here again, try to meet me on the other side of Jordan." It *was* our last earthly meeting.

Colonel Claiborne accompanied us to the cars, where we found we were to be escorted by a detachment of Morgan's celebrated guerillas. Claiborne gave orders for our humane treatment, saying: "They are men, like other men, and gentlemen too, and I want them treated as such." When he left, I felt we had parted from a friend, rebel as he was.

Claiborne's parting charge procured us courtesy from our guard. Indeed, they were a much better class of men than the great mass of the Southern army. Several of them told us that they had enlisted with Morgan only to make money, and were getting it fast. All were well dressed in citizens' clothes, and had the language and manners of gentlemen. They had another motive in treating us kindly. A large number of their own band were now in the hands of the government, and were equally liable with ourselves, under every rule of right, to be treated as criminals; for they had not only dressed in citizens' clothes, but had even assumed our uniform wherever it was their interest to do so. They were indignant to see us in irons, and said they would not be afraid to guard us with our limbs free, but did not, of course, dare to remove our fastenings.

We had been started as usual, without any rations, on the calculation that we should fast till we reached our destination, which would be in about twenty-four hours. But our guerilla friends would not permit this. They bought pies, and literally feasted us, saying that their money was plenty, and when it was gone they could easily get more from our men. We hoped that we might have Morgan's men for our escort in all future migrations.

We arrived in Knoxville shortly after noon, and marched through the hot, dusty streets, directly to the old jail. This is now a historical edifice. It will forever remain associated with the extreme sufferings of the loyal East Tennesseeans, during the progress of the great rebellion.

The building itself is a noble one, and resembles some old baronial hall. It is of a peculiar style of architecture—solid, square and massive, with lofty projecting towers and sharp angles—altogether presenting an imposing appearance. It was used as a military prison, and was filled from top to bottom with ragged, dirty-looking prisoners. Some were Union men, and others were deserters from their own rebel ranks. These constituted the *lower* class of prisoners, and were permitted to range over most of the building, which was completely encircled outside by a strong guard.

The higher class, or those who were charged with more desperate offences, were shut up in cages. There were five of these. Two of them were at once cleared for our reception. The smaller one was about seven feet by nine, and four of us were put into it. The larger, in which the remainder of the party were placed, was perhaps ten by twelve. The latter was the cage in which Parson Brownlow had been confined, and we felt honored by being in the same cell that this noble champion of the Union had once occupied.

While in this cage, we read an article in a copy of the *Knoxville Register*, stating that Brownlow was in the North, humbugging the Yankees by telling them that he had been kept in an iron cage, and fired at by his guards, when everybody in that vicinity knew that the whole thing was a falsity. Even while we read this, we looked at the shot-marks which were still visible on the cage, and which the guards and prisoners assured us had been made in the way Brownlow stated. This may serve as a specimen of the manner in which Southern papers are accustomed to deal with facts.

It was in the latter part of May when we arrived in Knoxville, and *outside*, the weather was intensely warm, but *inside*, from the enormous masses of stone and iron around, it was quite cool. Indeed the nights, which are always cool, even in midsummer, in the warmest parts of the South, were here very cold, and as we had no beds or blankets, but had to lie on the partly iron floor, we suffered greatly.

Here we formed the acquaintance of a few Tennesseeans, who continued with us during the remainder of our sojourn in Dixie. One of the most remarkable of their number was named Pierce. He was some sixty years old, and had received a stroke with a gun-barrel, right down his forehead, which, even after healing, had left a gash more than an inch deep. From this he was denominated, "Gun-barrel," "Forked head," &c. He was at the same time very religious and very profane. His voice would first be heard singing hymns, and next cursing the Confederacy in no measured terms. He was, however, a very clever man, and almost adored the name of a Union soldier.

Here it was that we first became acquainted with Captain Fry. He was confined in a cage in another room. We could not get to see him, but could entrust little notes, written on the margin of newspapers, to the more faithful of the outside prisoners, and were always sure of a reply.

There was one man in the same room with me, but in another cage, in whom I became especially interested. He was between seventy and eighty years old, and was awaiting sentence of death. Before his arrest he had been a Union man, and, of course, a marked object of suspicion to his secession neighbors. A band of these came one night for the purpose of robbing him. He endeavored to prevent them, when they attacked him, drawing revolvers and bowie-knives. They fired several shots, and pursued him. He dodged around old barrels and other pieces of furniture in the outhouse where the assault was made, for some time, until finally he managed to seize a pitch-fork and plunge it into the foremost of his foes; then breaking away, he escaped for the time. The robber whom he wounded afterwards died, and the Confederate government arrested the old man, and confined him in the cage on a charge of murder! I never heard the result of it, but have no doubt that he has long since been hung.

We obtained quite a number of papers while here, and were much pleased to learn of the continued progress of our arms, particularly in the West. The taking of Fort Pillow, the evacuation of Memphis and Corinth, with the destruction of the rebel flotilla on the Mississippi, all came out in one paper; and the editor complained that he had been restrained from publishing this by the government for more than two weeks after the intelligence arrived.

One day we received news that sent the blood coursing through our veins in swifter flow. It was that Andrews and one other of our party *had escaped from Chattanooga!*

Here, to preserve the unity of the story, I will give a history of the events that took place at Chattanooga subsequent to our departure.

No unusual event occurred until a week after we had left. Then, one day, an officer entered the yard, where our boys were enjoying the shade of the prison, in the cool of the afternoon, and carelessly handed to Andrews his *death-warrant!* It was a terrible shock, but was borne bravely. He communicated the startling intelligence to our comrades as soon as they again assembled in their room. At once they resolved to carry into immediate execution the long-projected plan of escape, on which now depended their leader's only chance of life.

He was separated from them, and put down into the dungeon. But this did not interfere with their plans, for with the same knife which was so serviceable in making keys, a hole was cut above the bolts of the trap-door, allowing it to be raised. This done, which was late at night, they drew Andrews up by blankets, and then went to work cutting another hole through the ceiling. While they were performing the most noisy part of this operation, they deadened the sound by singing. The jailor afterward remarked that he might have known there was something the matter by their singing so mournfully.

When all their preparations were completed, the gray tint of dawn was just beginning to rise in the east. There was no time to lose. Andrews quickly mounted aloft. A rope was formed of some twisted blankets, and the next moment he was swinging outside of the wall. But in passing through the hole he loosened some bricks which fell to the ground, and thus gave the alarm. The accident caused him to drop his boots, which he afterward sorely needed.

The guard was instantly aroused, but Andrews dropped to the ground, darted to the fence, and was over before he could be prevented. John Wollam followed, and even while suspended in the air by the blankets, was fired upon. Fortunately, the hands of the guards were too unsteady to inflict any injury, and he, too, succeeded in getting out of the yard in safety.

Now the excitement became intense. All Chattanooga was roused, and the whole force started in pursuit of the flying fugitives. The officers hurried to the prison and roundly berated our boys because they did not give the alarm when their comrades were escaping! Colonel Claiborne, the Marshal, who had shown us some humanity, was summarily dismissed from his office for that cause alone! And the press came out in the most violent language, denouncing the officers in charge, and particularly General Leadbetter, for their false philanthropy in not having us chained to the floor in such a manner as to make escape impossible.

Our flying comrades had separated as soon as they left the prison. It was now daylight, and they could not continue their flight without the most imminent danger of discovery. Andrews went only a few hundred yards from town, and there secreted himself in a tree, in plain view of the railroad. He remained all day in this uncomfortable position, and saw the trains running under his feet, and heard his pursuers speculating as to what course he could have taken. The search was most thorough; but, fortunately, his umbrageous shelter was secure.

At night he came down and swam the river, but lost most of his clothing in the passage; he then journeyed on nearly naked. In the morning, just at the break of day, he crossed a small open field on his way to a tree, in which he intended to take shelter, as he had done the day before; but, unfortunately, he was observed. Immediately pursuit was made, but he dashed through the woods, and regained the river, much lower down than he had crossed the evening before. Here he swam a narrow channel, and reached a small island, where, for a time, he secreted himself among some driftwood at the upper end of the island.

A party with bloodhounds now came over from the mainland in search of him. He was soon observed, but broke away from them, and ran around the lower end of the island, wading in the shallow water, and in this way threw the hounds off his track; then he plunged into a dense thicket, with which the island was covered, and again ascended a tree. There, for a long time, he remained securely concealed, while his pursuers searched the whole island, being frequently under the very tree whose high foliage effectually screened him from the sight of dogs and men. At last they abandoned the search in despair, concluding that he had, by some means, left the island, and slowly took their departure to the shore to concert new plans of search. Two little boys, who came along merely for curiosity, were all that still lingered behind.

At length, in their childish prattle, one of them said he saw a great bunch on a tree. The other looked—shifted his position—looked again, and exclaimed that it was *a man!* This alarmed them both, and they called aloud, announcing the discovery to their friends on shore. The latter instantly returned, and Andrews, seeing himself observed, dropped from the tree, ran to the lower end of the island, took a small log, with a limb for a paddle, and shoved into the stream, hoping to reach the opposite shore before he could be overtaken. But there was another party with a skiff, lower down the river, who saw him, and rowed out to meet him. Thus enclosed, there was no hope, and he surrendered.

He was in a most wretched condition, having eaten nothing since he left the jail. His feet were all cut and bleeding from running over the sharp stones, and his back and shoulders were parched and blistered from exposure, unprotected, to the rays of the sun. He said he felt so miserable that the thought of the certain death, to which he then resigned himself, had no further terror for him.

He was brought back to Chattanooga, where a blacksmith welded a pair of heavy clevises on his ankles, and connected them with a chain only about eighteen inches in length. He had then but few more days to live, and his confinement was most rigid. They prepared a scaffold for him at Chattanooga, but the indications of an advance by Mitchel, induced them to change the death scene to

Atlanta. All the way down to that place he was taunted with his approaching doom by the mobs who surrounded every station. Our eight comrades accompanied him to Atlanta, but parted as soon as they arrived—they going to prison, and he to the place of execution. He was compelled to walk, all ironed as he was, and the clanking of his chains no doubt made sweet music in the ears of these human bloodhounds.

He displayed great firmness when led to the place of execution, and mounted the scaffold without a tremor. When swung off, the rope by which he was suspended, stretched so that his feet came to the ground, but, nothing disconcerted, these wretches dug the earth away from under him and completed the murder! Thus died a good and brave man, at the early age of thirty-three, by the hands of rebels, for the crime of loving and trying to serve his country! He was engaged to be married to a young lady of his own adopted State the same month in which he suffered death on the scaffold!

It is now time to return to Wollam, whom we left outside of the jail-fence, trying to get away from Chattanooga.

He ran down to the river side, and seeing no way of crossing himself, hit on the brilliant ruse of making them believe that he was across. To this end he threw off his coat and vest, dropping them on the bank of the river, and then, after walking a few rods in the water to elude the hounds, quietly slipped back, and hid in a dense thicket of canes and rushes. He heard his pursuers on the bank above him, and all around, talking of their various plans. At last they found the clothes, and at once concluded that he had taken to the river. Then they took the bloodhounds over to the other side, and searched for the place of his exit from the water. The dogs could not find that, as might be expected, and then, after a due time spent in consultation, they concluded that he was drowned, and departing much comforted, searched no more for him.

After spending a day of most anxious suspense, the approach of night gave him an opportunity of leaving his hiding-place. He now cautiously made his way down the river on the Chattanooga side. At length he found a canoe, in which he rowed at night, and when morning came, he would sink it, and hide in the bushes; then in the evening raise it, and again pursue his way. Twice he passed the extempore gun-boat Mitchel had made, but feared it was some secession craft, and therefore crept cautiously by in the shadow of the shore, without being discovered. At last he thought he was beyond the danger of probable capture, and went boldly forward in the day time.

This was a fatal mistake. A band of cavalry, who were camped almost within our lines, saw him, and procuring a boat, came out to meet him. He was unable to escape, and thus the poor fellow was captured on the very brink of safety. He at first tried to persuade them that he was a Confederate, but, unfortunately, a Lieutenant Edwards, who had assisted in capturing him the first time, happened to be present, and at once recognized him. He was soon after taken to Atlanta, where the rest of the party then were.

Chapter 10
Placed on Trial

We, who were at Knoxville, read of the recapture of Andrews with the most poignant regret, though we knew not yet that he had received the sentence of death. Of Wollam we heard nothing.

We were well supplied with papers here, as there were plenty of Union people who ministered to our wants. One day we received a paper containing an account of the *execution of Andrews*. It was awful news to us. We had been engaged, just before, in all kinds of games and story-telling, for we were always merry, and never suffered ourselves to indulge in gloomy forebodings. But when this news came, all noise and merriment were hushed, and we passed a whole day in the most heartfelt mourning. We all loved our leader, and would willingly have engaged in the most desperate enterprise to save his life; but, alas! he was gone, and there was no chance even for that vengeance for which our souls thirsted.

Before we had been long at Knoxville, we were notified to prepare for trial. We requested that we should all be tried at once, as our cases were precisely alike. When this was not granted, we next asked that one might be tried, and his sentence be the sentence of the whole party. But this too, was refused, with the reply that they knew their own business best. We were forced to accept this decision, though we could not imagine why it was that they should thus insist on trying but one at a time. The only reason that I can yet conjecture for this proceeding is, that it would have looked too absurd to arraign twenty-one, or even twelve men, all in a body, and from one brigade, as spies.

They allowed us the privilege of counsel, and we employed two good Union men, Colonels Baxter and Temple, who volunteered their services. We were each to pay them one hundred and fifty dollars, and as fast as we were tried, to give our notes for that amount.

The charges and specifications of William Campbell were first handed in. He was a citizen, but claimed to be a soldier, and we endorsed his position. The charge against all who were brought to trial was for "lurking in and around Confederate camps as spies, for the purpose of obtaining information." Not a word was said of taking the cars, or of anything we really did do.

Our plan of defence has been partly indicated before. It was to tell just who we were, and what we had done, with the exceptions of the pranks we had played on the rebel citizens coming down, and to claim that we were United States soldiers, detailed on a military expedition without our consent, and therefore entitled to the protection accorded to regular prisoners of war. This was put into words, and read on the trial as the acknowledgement of the party while pleading "not guilty" to the charge. The only evidence they had was of the men who pursued us on the train, and also of those who afterward arrested us; but of course none of these knew anything of our lurking around the camps.

George D. Wilson related a ludicrous incident that occurred when he was on trial, and which fitly illustrates the desire they had to convict us. It was of a young lieutenant belonging to the court-martial, who requested to be sworn, saying that he could tell of at least one place we had passed the Confederate guards. On his request being complied with, he testified that we crossed their picket-line at the ferry, on the evening of our first arrival at Chattanooga. Immediately the president of the court arose, and said that he commanded the guard that day, and *no guard was placed at the ferry.* The whole court was instantly in a roar of laughter, and the confusion of our would-be convictor may be better imagined than described.

Our lawyers were delighted with the course we took, and said that it had deranged all the plans of the prosecution, and that they had not a particle of evidence against us; that if we were convicted now, it would be through mere prejudice and perjury on the part of the court.

As the trial of different ones proceeded, we had still greater encouragement from the court itself. Members called on us, and told us to keep in good heart, as there was no evidence before them to convict any one. This cheered us somewhat, but there was still one thing which I did not like, and which looked as if something was wrong. The court would not let our boys be present to hear the pleading of counsel on either side, though they urgently requested it. They could neither hear what our lawyers had to say for them, nor what the Judge Advocate urged against them. This seemed still stranger, because Andrews had not been debarred this privilege. But they used our soldiers with even less show of justice than had been accorded to him.

After three or four had been tried, one of our lawyers visited the prison, and read to us the plea which he said he had read to the court. It was an able paper. I still remember its principal features. He contended that our being dressed in citizens' clothes was nothing more than what the Confederate government had expressly authorized, and that it was done by all the guerillas in the service of the Confederacy, whenever it was for their interest. And he cited the instance of General Morgan having dressed his men in Federal uniform, and passed them off as belonging to the Eighth Pennsylvania Cavalry, by which means he succeeded in reaching a railroad and damaging it. Also that our government had captured some of these very men, and treated them as prisoners of war. This instance was mentioned to show that our being dressed in citizens' clothes did not take from us the right to be treated as United States soldiers. The plea went on further to state that we had told the object of our expedition; that it was a purely military one, for the destruction of communications, and as such, entirely lawful according to the rules of war. What reply the Judge Advocate made to this, we never had the means of ascertaining.

The trials proceeded rapidly. One man was taken out each day, and in about an hour returned. The table in the court room was covered with bottles, newspapers, and novels, and the court passed its time during trial in discussing these. This was very well if the trial was, as they said, a mere matter of formality; but if it was a trial in earnest, on which depended issues of life or death, it was most heartless conduct.

At last the number of seven was reached, and they would probably have proceeded in trying others, had not General Mitchel, who was continually troubling them, now advanced, and shelled Chattanooga from the opposite side of the Tennessee river. This at once broke up the court-martial, and sent the officers in hot haste to their regiments to resist his progress. Soon after, General Morgan advanced through Cumberland Gap, and threatened Knoxville, which also rendered it necessary to remove us.

They came in with ropes and began to tie us. We did not at first understand this, and some supposed we were to be taken out for execution; but we soon became convinced that it was only a change of place. They arranged us for transportation by first binding our hands together; then, fixing our arms securely in the loops of long ropes, tied them firmly to our sides, after which we were coupled two and two. Ropes were used in fastening us instead of irons as before, because they had borrowed the latter for some Union prisoners, who had just been sent to Richmond; therefore we had to be content with a most liberal allowance of cotton rope. While they were thus arranging our manacles, I had a most amusing passage-at-words with the adjutant who was superintending the operation. I said to him as politely as I could:

"I suppose, sir, our destination is not known?"

"It is not known to you at any rate, sir," was the gruff rejoinder.

This was noticed by the whole party, and I felt rather beaten; but a moment later came my chance for revenge. He turned again to me, and said, in a dictatorial manner:

"Who was it that run your engine through?"

I bowed and returned in the blandest tone, *"That is not known to you at any rate, Sir."*

All around roared with laughter, and the adjutant, reddening to the eyes, turned away, muttering that he believed I was the engineer myself!

When everything was in readiness, we bade an adieu to the capital of down-trodden East Tennessee. Oh! what bitter memories cluster around that old gloomy building. It has been one of the principal instruments in crushing the life and loyalty out of the hearts of a brave, but unfortunate people. May the day soon come when the suffering of East Tennessee will be richly repaid on the heads of its guilty authors!

While we remained here, our fare was of the most scanty character. We received it only twice a day, and then in homeopathic doses. We continually suffered with hunger while we were well. I, myself, became quite sick during our imprisonment here, and continued so for most of the summer. Several others were in the same condition. This was rather an advantage, for when sick we did not so much mind the scantiness of our diet.

A number of Tennesseeans were removed with us. Among them was Captain Fry and Mr. Pierce. In conversation with the former, I learned the full particulars of his history, some incidents of which I had heard before leaving our camp. He had raised a company of his neighbors, and running the gauntlet of guarded roads, succeeded in reaching our army in Kentucky. Here he was elected captain, and remained for some time. After a while, the general in command wished him to go into Tennessee, and there destroy the bridges on the Virginia and Tennessee Railroad; then to raise the loyal citizens of that vicinity, and hold the country till our forces could arrive. He refused to go, until assured of support from McClellan himself, who was at that time (the fall of 1861) in command of the whole United States army, and who promised that a column should advance as soon as Fry succeeded. With this assurance, he departed on his perilous mission. He aroused the Union men in both Virginia and Tennessee, burned the bridges, and thus for a time destroyed the most important rebel line of communication; and, with a force of fifteen hundred men, held the entire country embraced in his operations, and even seriously threatened Knoxville itself. Now was the time for our forces to have struck the decisive blow, and not only have redeemed East Tennessee from its chains, but also severed the rebellion in halves! It was perfectly practicable. A large body lay near Camp Dick Robinson, with only a trifling force in front to impede its progress. But in the meantime, McClellan *had changed his plans*, and without warning Fry, left him and his brave companions to their fate. The struggle was a brief one; the secessionists, thus left to themselves, concentrated an overwhelming force against him. Several skirmishes were fought, and finally the Union force was compelled to disperse. Some of them succeeded in reaching our lines in Kentucky. Others were caught, and several of these were hung without a trial! Such were some of the murders that first rendered General Leadbetter notorious!

One of these cases is almost too horrible for belief. I would hesitate to record it, were I not assured of its truth by the testimony of eyewitnesses separated by hundreds of miles. It was of a man named named Whan, who, on being arrested, acknowledged that he helped to burn the bridges, but refused to describe his companions. For this, he was put into a barrel driven full of small, sharp-pointed nails, and rolled down a steep hill—then taken out, all bleeding, and hung! This was on Saturday and he, with his companions, was allowed to hang till Monday night, when some of his friends, at the risk of their own lives, came and took them down! Should we compromise with such fiends in human shape, and purchase their fellowship again, or give them the puishment that injured humanity demands?

Fry passed the whole winter in the wild mountains with which Tennessee abounds, and in the spring he again gathered his neighbors together, a regiment strong, and tried to reach the Union lines. Near the border, he was attacked by a superior rebel force, and after a severe contest, his band was dispersed, himself wounded and taken prisoner. This was on the 5th of March, and he remained in solitary confinement until he joined us on the 13th of June. He was an uneducated man, but possessed of great natural ability, and the most undaunted courage, with a heart as tender and sympathetic as a child's.

We took no rations along, and were obliged to *starve through*, as we now had no guerillas along to buy us pies. On the way, the populace taunted us with Andrews' death, and charitably hoped that we might soon meet the same fate. But some of the officers talked with us in a friendly spirit, assuring us that we would not be hurt. This produced some impression, and taken in connection with what had been told us by members of the court-martial, and others at Knoxville, made us quite hopeful.

When we neared the Atlanta city jail, which was to be our abode for many weary months, a crowd gathered as usual, and a man who called himself mayor of the city began to insult Captain Fry, telling him that he knew him to be a rascal in his own country, and that he hoped soon to have the pleasure of hanging him. Then turning to us, he boasted that he had put the rope around Andrews' neck, and was waiting and anxious to do the same for us!

This prison was smaller than that at Knoxville, but was still a large edifice. The lower story was occupied by the jailor and his family. The upper contained four rooms, of which we, with Captain Fry, occupied one. The Tennesseeans were put into another, just across the entry from us. Our comrades, who had been left at Chattanooga, were in another; and the last one, which was on the same side as ours, was frequently occupied by negroes who had been in search of the North Star.

For some time here, our rations were comparatively good and abundant. But after awhile, the task of feeding us was taken from the jailor, who had at first assumed it, and then our fare became worse than it ever had been before. The jailor himself was a kind man, and rather of Union sentiments. He showed us all the favor in his power, and, indeed, became so much suspected, that an odious old man named Thoer was hired to watch him. The constant vigilance of this antiquated scoundrel, with the superintendence of the officers of the guard, who were always at hand, prevented the jailor from befriending us as much as his heart dictated.

Here we remained for a week in quietness and hope, thinking the worst of our trials were past. Little did we foresee how fearful a storm was soon to burst over us.

Chapter 11

Death Upon the Scaffold

One day while we were very merry, amusing ourselves with games and stories, we saw a squadron of cavalry approaching. This did not at first excite any attention, for it was a common thing to see bodies of horsemen in the streets; but soon we observed them halt at our gate, and surround the prison. What could this mean?

A moment after, the clink of the officers' swords was heard as they ascended the stairway, and we knew that something unusual was about to take place. They paused at our door, threw it open, called the names of our seven companions, and took them out to the room opposite, putting the Tennesseeans in with us. One of our boys, named Robinson, was sick of a fever, and had to be raised to his feet, and supported out of the room.

With throbbing hearts we asked one another the meaning of these strange proceedings. Some supposed they were to receive their acquittal; others, still more sanguine, believed they were taken out of the room to be paroled, preparatory to an exchange.

I was sick, too, but rose to my feet, oppressed with a nameless fear. A half crazy Kentuckian, who was with the Tennesseeans, came to me and wanted to play a game of cards. I struck the greasy pack out of his hands, and bade him leave me.

A moment after, the door opened, and George D. Wilson entered, his step firm and his form erect, but his countenance pale as death. Some one asked a solution of the dreadful mystery, in a whisper, for his face silenced every one.

"*We are to be executed immediately,*" was the awful reply, whispered with thrilling distinctness. The others came in all tied, ready for the scaffold. Then came the farewells—farewells with no hope of meeting again in this world! It was a moment that seemed an age of measureless sorrow.

Our comrades were brave; they were soldiers, and had often looked death in the face on the battle-field. They were ready, if need be, to die for their country; but to die on the *scaffold*—to die as murderers die—seemed almost too hard for human nature to bear.

Then, too, the prospect of a future world, into which they were thus to be hurled without a moment's preparation, was black and appalling. Most of them had been careless, and had no hope beyond the grave. Wilson was a professed infidel, and many a time had argued the truth of the Christian religion with me for a half day at a time; but in this awful hour he said to me:

"Pittenger, I believe you are right, now! Oh! try to be better prepared when you come to die than I am." Then, laying his hand on my head with a muttered "God bless you," we parted.

Shadrack was profane and reckless, but good-hearted and merry. Now, turning to us with a voice, the forced calmness of which was more affecting than a wail of agony, he said:

"Boys, I am not prepared to meet Jesus."

When asked by some of us in tears to think of heaven, he answered, still in tones of thrilling calmness, "I'll try! I'll try! But I *know* I am *not* prepared."

Slavens, who was a man of immense strength and iron resolution, turned to his friend Buffum, and could only articulate, "Wife—children—tell"—when utterance failed.

Scott was married only three days before he came to the army, and the thought of his young and sorrowing wife nearly drove him to despair. He could only clasp his hands in silent agony.

Ross was the firmest of all. His eyes beamed with unnatural light, and there was not a tremor in his voice as he said, "Tell them at home, if any of you escape, that I died for my country, and did not regret it."

All this transpired in a moment, and even then the Marshal and other officers standing by him in the door, exclaimed:

"Hurry up there! come on! we can't wait!"

In this manner my poor comrades were hurried off. Robinson, who was too sick to walk, was dragged away with them. They asked leave to bid farewell to our other boys, who were confined in the adjoining room, but it was sternly refused!

Thus we parted. We saw the death cart containing our comrades drive off, surrounded by cavalry. In about an hour it came back *empty*. The tragedy was complete!

Later in the evening, the Provost-Marshal came to the prison, and, in reply to our questions, informed us that our friends "Had met their fate as brave men should die everywhere."

The next day we obtained from the guards, who were always willing to talk with us in the absence of the officers, full particulars of the seven-fold murder.

When our companions were mounted on the scaffold, Wilson asked permission to say a few words, which was granted—probably in the hope of hearing some confession which would justify them in the murder they were about to commit. But this was not his intention. It was a strange stand—a dying speech to a desperate audience, and under the most terrible circumstances.

But he was equal to the occasion. Unterrified by the near approach of death, he spoke his mind freely. He told them that "they were all in the wrong; that he had no hard feelings toward the Southern people for what they were about to do, because they had been duped by their leaders, and induced by them to engage in the work of rebellion. He also said, that though he was condemned as a spy, yet he was none, and they well knew it. He was only a soldier in the performance of the duty he had been detailed to do; that he did not regret to die for his country, but only regretted the manner of his death. He concluded by saying that they would yet live to regret the part they had taken in this rebellion, and would see the time when the old Union would be restored, and the flag of our country wave over the very ground occupied by his scaffold."

This made a deep impression on the minds of those who listened, and I often afterward heard it spoken of in terms of the highest admiration. When he ceased, the signal was given, and the traps fell![4]

Five only remained dangling in the air; for two of the seven, Campbell and Slavens, being very heavy men, broke the ropes, and fell to the ground insensible. In a short time they recovered, and asked for a drink of water, which was given them. Then they requested an hour to pray before entering the future world which lay so near and dark before them. This last petition was indignantly refused, and as soon as the ropes could be adjusted, they were compelled to re-ascend the scaffold, and were again turned off!

---

4. A refugee from the State of Georgia, now in this city, who witnessed the execution, but, from peculiar circumstances, does not make his name public, corroborates this statement, and adds, that these brave men were surrounded by three or four hundred guerrillas and partisan rangers, as they called themselves, who disputed for the honour of being the executioners. The matter was settled by the party taking a vote, when twelve were selected as the favoured ones. The rebel soldiers who perpetrated this outrageous murder, spent the rest of the day in spreeing and jollification, many of them writing to their friends at home an account of the pleasure they felt in assisting in the hanging of "seven blue-bellies," as they termed the Union soldiers.—*Note from a Pamphlet entitled "Ohio Boys in Dixie," published in New York in April, 1863.*

The whole proceeding, from beginning to end, was marked by the most revolting haste. They seemed to wish, by thus affording no time to prepare for death, to murder soul and body both. Even the worst criminals in our country are allowed some weeks to ask for God's mercy, before they are thrust into his presence; but our poor boys, whose only crime was loving and trying to serve their country, were not allowed one moment! Could the barbarity of fiends go further?

That afternoon was one of deepest gloom for those who remained. We knew not how soon we might be compelled to follow in the same path, and drink the same bitter cup our comrades drank. Once during the trial we had offered to accept the award of the court in one of the cases as the sentence of all, since we could not see the slightest reason for leaving some and taking others. At that time, however, we believed that all would be acquitted. Now every hope had vanished.

But even without the addition of fear for ourselves, the parting from our loved friends, whose voices were still ringing in our ears, while they themselves had passed beyond the gates of death into the unknown land of shadows, was enough to rend the stoutest heart. There were tears then from eyes that shrank before no danger.

But I could not shed a tear. A cloud of burning heat rushed to my head that seemed to scorch through every vein. For hours I scarcely knew where I was, or the loss I had sustained. Every glance around the room, which revealed the vacant places of our friends, would bring our sorrow freshly on us again. Thus the afternoon passed away in grief too deep for words. Slowly and silently the moments wore on, and no one ventured to whisper of hope.

At last some voice suggested that we should seek relief in prayer. The very idea seemed to convey consolation, and was eagerly accepted. Soon we knelt around the bare walls of our strange sanctuary, and with bleeding hearts drew near the throne of God. Captain Fry first led us, and mingled sobs with strong supplications. Then each followed in his turn, with but one or two exceptions, and even these were kneeling with the rest. As the twilight deepened, our devotional exercises grew more solemn. In the lonely shadow of coming night, with eternity thus open tangibly before us, and standing on its very brink, we prayed with a fervour that those who dwell in safety can scarcely conceive. We besought our Father only that we might be prepared for the fate that was inevitable, and that as he had led us through great trials, he would be our Comforter, and sustain us still. Who will say that such prayer was not effectual! It was heard in heaven. Even there, in that prison, surrounded by an armed guard, amid the gloom of coming danger, the peace of God, like a dove bearing the olive branch, descended into every broken and believing heart. It was a holy hour, and if the angels above ever bend from their bright mansions to comfort human sorrow, I do believe that they were then hovering near. From that hour I date the birth of an immortal hope, and I believe that many of my companions also, on looking back, will realize that they passed from death to life in that dreary prison-room!

Chapter 12

Prisoner of the Confederacy

From this time forward, we had religious exercises each morning and evening, and they were a blessed consolation to us—sustaining our hearts when every earthly avenue of hope had closed. Frequently we startled the guards who were around us, by the hymns we sang, for now the character of our songs was changed, and our thoughts and aspirations began to point upward. It is a delicate matter to speak of one's own religious experience, but in the hope of doing good, I will venture. At first my hopes were not bright. For days and weeks an impenetrable cloud seemed to rest over me, and to veil heaven from my view; sometimes for a moment it would give way, and show light and peace beyond, then close up, thick, and dark, and lowering, as ever. But at last the day gradually arose, and I was enabled to rejoice in hopes the world can neither give nor take away.

But these were long and weary days. Our room was of greater size than that in Chattanooga, and had larger windows, yet the heat was fearfully oppressive. Our other boys were put in the room with us, which made fifteen in all. One of them, named Wood, was very sick. He had been prostrated with the fever for nearly a month, and at this time his life was despaired of. This was not thought to be any great misfortune to him by the others, who administered consolation in a style worthy of the best of Job's friends. They reasoned, "Now, if you get well, you will only be hung. You had better try to die yourself, and thus you will outwit them." Wood, however, did not relish the counsel, and getting contrary, he recovered, "just for spite," as he often declared. He yet lives to laugh over the advice that his despairing associates gave him.

We had friends in the waiters of the prison, though their faces were black. They assisted us by every means in their power. It was not long till they found that there was nothing we desired so much as to read the news; and they taxed their ingenuity to gratify us. They would wait till the jailor or some of the guard had finished reading a paper, and laid it down, and then slyly purloin it. When meal time came, it would be put into the bottom of the pan in which our food was brought, and thus handed in to us. The paper had to be returned in the same way, to avoid suspicion.[5] The guards and officers would talk with us, and always finding us possessed of a knowledge of the events of the war, at least as far as the Southern papers gave it, came at last to think we had an instinctive idea of news—something like what the bee has of geometrical forms! They never suspected the negroes, though for several months it was only through their instrumentality that we could obtain any definite information of what was going on in the world without.

Having found the negroes thus intelligent and useful, far beyond what I had supposed possible, I questioned them about other matters. They were better informed than I had given them credit for, and knew enough to disbelieve all the stories rebels told. When the whites were not present, they laughed at the grand victories the papers were publishing every day, but rather leaned to the opposite extreme, and gave them less credit than was their due, for they would believe that the Federal troops were always victorious. Even after McClellan's repulse before Richmond, they continued, for weeks, to assure us that he had the town, and had beaten the rebels in every engagement!

They imagined that all the Northern troops were chivalrous soldiers, fighting for the universal rights of man, and, of course, they esteemed it a high privilege to contribute to the comfort of such noble men. Some of them had imbibed the idea, which is common with the poor whites of the South, that Lincoln is a negro or a mulatto; but most of them placed so little credit in the assertions of their masters, that they disbelieved this story also. But they never wavered in their belief that the Union troops would conquer, and that the result of the victory would be their freedom. I had extensive opportunities for observing them, as the room next to us was appropriated to the safe-keeping of negroes, and I never yet saw one who did not cherish an ardent desire for freedom, and wish and long for the time when the triumph of the national forces would place the coveted boon within his grasp.

One morning our jailor came to our room, and asked us if we knew John Wollam. We hesitated to answer, as we could not fathom

---

5. In one of these papers I noticed a description of two Federal officers who had escaped from Macon, Georgia. It was Captain Geer, with whom I have lectured in several places since my return, and his comrade, Lieutenant Collins. Their adventures are recorded in a book called *Beyond the Lines*.

the motives of the inquiry. But even while we deliberated among ourselves, John came up, and ended our doubts by greeting us heartily. He had been parted from us some three weeks, and in that time had suffered most incredible hardships in the manner I have narrated before. He joined us in our prayer-meeting with much good will. Now all the survivors of our party were together again.

There is one Georgia minister I will always remember with gratitude, not that he was a Union man, for I have no evidence that he was, but because of his generosity to us. He was a Methodist clergyman in Atlanta, by the name of McDonnell. He came to visit us at the suggestion of our old jailor, who, seeing us engaged in religious exercises, naturally supposed we would like to talk with a preacher. We received him kindly, and an interesting conversation took place. Some of the boys were slightly offended by his first prayer, in which he petitioned that our lives might be spared, if consistent with the *interests of the Confederacy*. We did not very well like the condition, but said nothing, and were afterward rewarded for our complacency. At my request, he loaned us a few books, and when these were read through, gave us still others, until we had read nearly his entire library. Those only who know what a terrible weariness it is to pass time without any definite employment, and with no means of relieving the hours that hang so heavily on their hands, or of diverting their thoughts from the one never-ending round, can form any idea of the great boon that a few good books bestowed on us.

Our provision here became worse and less, until it very nearly reached the starvation point. For some months, the only food we received was a very short allowance of corn-bread, baked with all the bran in it, and without salt, with a little pork, mostly spoiled! Frequently the pork would be completely covered with maggots, and disgusting as it was, hunger compelled us to eat it! Even then, there was not enough of this miserable fare to satisfy our appetites! What would those who spend their time in denouncing our government as the only enemy, and sympathize with "our mistaken Southern brethren," who have been alienated by the misconduct of the loyal States, say, if these "brethren" had subjected them to the same treatment. Their sympathies would hardly have survived the trial.

Dreary as the days were here, yet we did not surrender ourselves to gloomy forebodings and vain lamentings over our misfortunes. Although the fate of our companions seemed suspended over our heads by a single hair, yet we shunned despondency, and laboured to provide such amusements as would relieve us of the heavy tedium of our prison-life.

On that terrible day of execution, we threw away our cards, which before had been played almost day and night, and resolved to engage no more in that game. But the necessity of doing something prompted us to search for new pastimes. We carved a checker-board on the floor, and it was occupied from morning till evening by eager players. We all became very expert in checkers. To provide a more intellectual amusement, we also formed a debating society, and spent hour after hour in discussing quaint questions of every kind. Many were the long-winded speeches that were made, for time was no object; and if no one was convinced of a new position, we still had the consolation of knowing that there was no lost labour, where the labour itself was a pleasure.

In order to enjoy to the fullest extent the books we had so fortunately procured, we appointed regular reading hours—two in the forenoon, and the same in the afternoon. During this time, no one was allowed even to whisper. Some of our boys were a little wild and restless at times, and would break the rules; but generally our order was excellent. We gained much useful knowledge during these hours of intellectual employment in our novel school.

But all our efforts to pleasantly while away those terribly long summer days were in vain. The tediousness, and oppressiveness, and vain longing for action, would press down on us closer and closer. Brown, who was one of the most restless of mortals, would amuse himself, as long as he could endure it, at the pastimes we had devised, then suddenly cease playing, and commence pacing the floor like a caged bear; when this, too, grew unendurable, he would stop at the door, and say, in the most piteous tones (of course meant only for us to hear) "O! kind sir, please let me out!" The feeling he expressed was shared by all. Never before could I realize the full value of liberty, and the horror of confinement. Even in the prisons where we had hitherto been, the novelty of our situation, the frequency of our removals, and the bustle and excitement of the trial, prevented the blank monotony of imprisonment from settling down on us as it did here, when the first few weeks had rolled by, and no intimations of our fate reached us. It was like the stillness and the death that brood over the Dead Sea.

We would sit at the windows, in the sultry noon, and look out through the bars, at the free birds as they flew past, seemingly so merry and full of joyous life, and foolishly wish that we, too, were birds, that we might fly away, and be at peace.

At long intervals, two of us would be permitted to go down into the yard, to do our washing. One day it came my turn; it was then three months since I had stepped out of my room, and the unobscured vision of open air and sky made it seem like another world. I remember looking up at the snowy clouds, my eyes almost dazzled by the unusual light, and wondering, as I gazed on their beautiful and changing forms, whether beyond them lay a world of rest, in which were neither wars nor prisons. And with the thought came the fear that if I was once more permitted to mingle as a free man, away from the immediate pressure of danger, with the busy throng of life, I would forget my prison-made vows, and thus lose my claim to a world of never-fading light. Such a sense of weakness and helplessness came over me, that it was with a feeling almost of relief that I returned once more to my dark and narrow room, where the contrast between freedom and bondage was less palpably forced on my view.

All this time we hardly permitted ourselves to indulge a hope of ever getting home again. The friends we once knew in happier days, seemed separated from us by an impassable gulf; and when our minds would call up before us the scenes and loved ones of home, it was like treading on forbidden ground. But when the miseries of the day were passed, and we were wrapped in that sweet slumber that ever visits the weary alike in prison and palace, there was no longer any restraint, and we were once more at home—once more in the enjoyment of love and freedom.

Often have I seen in dreams the streets and buildings of my own town rise before me, and have felt a thrilling pleasure in contemplating them, as I wended my way towards the sacred precincts for ever hallowed by affection. But the waking from these incursions into the realms of paradise was sad beyond measure, and the cold, bare walls of prison never looked half so dreary, as when seen in contrast with the visions which had just been dispersed by the morning light.

An anecdote here will fitly illustrate the affection and exaggerated reverence we felt for what we, to the great annoyance of the guards and citizens, insisted on calling "God's country." I had been reading one of Bascom's sermons, from a book which the minister had loaned us, on "The Joys of Heaven." All listened to his magnificent description with the greatest of interest, and when it was finished, some one started the query as to whether they would rather be in heaven, safe from all harm, or in Cincinnati. After a debate which was conducted with great animation on both sides, the majority concluded, no doubt honestly, that they would rather be in Cincinnati—for a while, at least!

In order to keep thoroughly posted, we opened communications to every room in the prison. Those on the other side of the entry, we reached by means of a small stick, attached to a string, and thrown under the door. There was a chimney came up between our room and the other on the same side of the entry; each of our stove-pipes led into this chimney at points directly opposite, and by taking off the pipes, we could talk through, but there was danger of being overheard. To obviate this, we split a long lath off the side of our room, in such a way as to be able to take it down and put it up at pleasure. This we used for passing notes backward and forward through this concealed passage, and it became very useful when we afterward contemplated an escape.

One morning the guard brought up some prisoners, and as soon as they had retired, we resorted to our usual method of telegraphing, to ascertain their character. To our great surprise and pleasure, we found that two of them were from the Tenth Wisconsin, a regiment in our own brigade. They told us that we had long since been given up for dead,[6] and that our comrades were vowing vengeance for our murder. They were quite surprised to find so many of us still alive. The other two were regulars, who had been captured on the coast of Florida. These soldiers remained with us till we were taken to Richmond. From them we gained a complete detail of the movements of our army since we had left it.

One of the hardest things we had to endure was the rejoicing that accompanied McClellan's flight from Richmond. Before this occurrence, the secessionists were down-spirited and despairing; but afterward they were jubilant. About the last of May, a prominent officer said to me: "Any other officer of yours but McClellan, would now take Richmond, for we have not men enough at present to offer successful resistance; but *he* will fortify each step of his way, and lay grand plans, and thus delay until we can raise men enough by the conscript law to defeat him." I did not then think that his prediction would be verified, and hoped that McClellan would show that he was not delaying for nothing; but when I heard of the precipitate retreat to Harrison's Landing, I was ready to confess that the Confederate officer had been more penetrating in his views than myself. From this moment, the tide of victory seemed to set to the southward side, with a still deeper and stronger flow, till the next spring, when it returned again.

I can preserve no order of time in relating the events of these tedious mouths, which slowly rolled away their ponderous length. It was almost a perfect isolation from the world, with little hope of ever again mingling in its busy throng. As each month closed, we were startled

---

6. All our friends at home believed we were executed. My obituary notice was published in our county paper, and the Rev. Alexander Clark was invited to preach my funeral sermon, which providential circumstances alone prevented.

by the thought we were still alive—that the bolt had not yet descended—and we surmised and wondered how much longer it could be delayed. At last a small ray of hope began to arise—very feeble at first—based on the long and incomprehensible reprieve we were enjoying. As week after week glided tediously away, marked only by the monotony which is more wearying to heart and frame than the most severe anguish, this hope grew stronger; yet still so little assured that the most trifling circumstance, such as strengthening the guard, or a visit from the officers, was sufficient to blast the hopes we were beginning so fondly to cherish.

I saw many instances of the iron rule with which the Southern Union men are kept in subjection. The strictest espionage was maintained through every order of society. The spies of the government would pretend to be Union men, and thus worm themselves into loyal societies; and when they had learned the names of the members, would denounce them to the government. It was not necessary to be particular about truth, as the suspicion of guilt, in their mode of procedure, was just as good as its positive evidence. One day seventy men and twelve women were arrested, and sent in irons to Richmond! Many other instances of this remorseless tyranny will be given hereafter.

Most of our boys were tobacco-chewers, and were driven to numberless expedients to obtain that which some of them declared they valued more than their daily food. There were several articles of which the rebels had not seen fit to rob us, such as handkerchiefs and a few vests; These were now sold to the surrounding guards. Andrews had given Hawkins a very large, fine coat, and as there seemed to be no prospect of taking it home, he sold it to the jailor, and invested the proceeds in tobacco, apples, &c., which he generously divided among his comrades.

I wanted books more than anything else, and sold my vest and a pocket-book the rebels had left when they took what was in it, and bought three books—all gems—*Paradise Lost*, *Pilgrim's Progress*, and Pollock's *Course of Time*. These I nearly committed to memory. It was a profitable employment, while I am sure it very much lightened and shortened these interminable days.

Chapter 13
Our Bid for Freedom

We frequently talked and plotted about making our escape. All agreed, that if they should proceed to try us, we should make one desperate effort for life; for we had learned by sad experience, that they did not take the trouble of going to the formality of a trial unless they were fully resolved to hang the accused. But as time rolled on, and the dreaded preparations for trial were not made, the imprisonment became daily more unendurable. The food was of a poorer quality, and more scanty at that. It was, therefore, proposed that we should make a bold strike for freedom. The question was a serious one. On the one hand was the bright prize of liberty—of which none ever knew the value better than we,—shining ahead as the sure reward of success. But on the other hand was the danger of failure. We were in the very centre of the Confederacy, and the nearest point where we could reach our lines was two hundred miles distant. This journey had to be made through the enemy's country, and by travelling at night, with no guide but the stars, which the envious clouds might conceal from us for many successive nights, as they had done before. Then there was the probability that those who were retaken would be mercilessly dealt with, if not instantly put to death.

It was a grave question. And then the great heat of the days, added to our enfeebled condition, caused by the close confinement, and the meagre character of our diet, as well as the actual sickness of some of our party, including myself, induced me to believe that the attempt should at least be postponed. Still, day by day, we discussed the subject. It afforded us an inexhaustible theme for conversation, and had this further advantage that all the knowledge possessed by the party collectively was communicated to each one. Besides, the plans were laid by which to avoid pursuit, and all possible information respecting the country obtained from the guards and negroes, and then we felt quite prepared for the issue when it should come.

At last we received a piece of intelligence which made us resolve to hesitate no longer. Colonel Lee, Provost-Marshal, came to our room one morning, and after talking some time, told us that he had just received a letter from the Secretary of War, asking why *all* the party had not been executed. He had answered that he did not know, but referred him to the court-martial which had tried our comrades at Knoxville. This court had dispersed long before, and I feel hopeful that many of the perjured villains have fallen beneath the avenging bullets of Union soldiers! So the Secretary could not have obtained much information from them. A few days after, we received still further and more alarming information.

One of the regular soldiers in the adjoining room overheard the officer of the guard telling the jailor that Colonel Lee had received another letter from the Secretary, ordering our immediate execution. This was duly telegraphed to us through the stove-pipe, and at once put an end to all our deliberations. The time had come for us to save ourselves or perish.

Quietly we sat down and arranged our plans. We were in an upper story, and several locked doors had to be opened before we could reach the ground. There were seven guards keeping watch over us, and a large force near by ready to rush to their assistance at the slightest notice. It was evident that our only chance of success lay in moving very quickly and silently. We could not leave at night, for then all the doors were closed, and we had no means of opening them. The best time was at supper, which was brought a little before sundown, and by starting then, we would soon have the cover of darkness to conceal our flight. The soldiers in the next room, and a deserter who was confined with them, agreed to go with us, if we would open their door. Only one of the Tennesseeans, named Barlow, would risk the trial, although they were anxious for the movement before it was seriously contemplated.

The plan on which we finally settled, was to seize the jailor when he came to take out the buckets in which our supper was brought, holding him so that he could make no noise, take the keys from him, and let Buffum unlock the doors and release the remaining prisoners. While this was being done, our other boys would divide into two squads, and, cautiously descending the stairway, pounce upon the guards, and take their guns from them; then, at a signal, we would all come down, and march, thus armed, on our homeward journey. We very nearly succeeded in our programme.

The second day after receiving the news, all our plans were completed. We had patched our clothes as best we could, and made cloth moccasins to protect our feet, for many of our shoes were altogether worn out. Now we only awaited the approach of the appointed hour. Slowly the sun rolled down the west; slowly the shadows lengthened in the east, till the gloomy shade of the jail had nearly reached the crest of the hill which usually marked our supper time. The eventful hour drew nigh. We bade one another a solemn farewell, for we knew not when we should meet again on earth, or how many of us might be cold and lifeless before the stars shone out. Captain Fry, who was tender-hearted as a child, wept at the parting. He had two coats, and, as he could not take both with him, he gave one to me. I needed it extremely, for I was very nearly destitute of clothing.

Everything was now in readiness. I had piled up the books of the minister, some of which we still retained, in the corner, and had written him a note thanking him for the use of them. We had on our coats, and had a few canes, and bottles, and pieces of lath, taken out of the wall, which were to be used in the fight down stairs, if necessary. Then came the supper. It was brought in by negroes, the jailor standing at the door. Our preparations for leaving were not noticed. We ate in silence, stowing part of the bread in our pockets for future emergencies. It so happened that the old watchman, whom everybody hated, was away. It was well for him, as he would have received little mercy.

After the jailor had given their food to the inmates of the other rooms, he came back to ours. We asked him to let Barlow come over and stay with us that night. He consented, and soon Barlow was with us. Now was the time for action.

It was a thrilling moment! On the action of the next few minutes hung the issues, probably, of life or death. I confess that for one moment the blood flowed to my heart with a sharp throb of pain. The others were pale, but determined. As for Captain Fry, who was to initiate the movement, and whom I had seen weeping a few minutes before—he was perfectly calm, and his face wore a pleasant smile. He stepped out of the door as if it was the most natural action in the world, and said, very quietly:

"A pleasant evening, Mr. Turner."

"Yes, rather pleasant," responded the latter, looking as if he could not understand what Fry was out there for.

"We feel like taking a little walk this evening," continued the captain. The astonishment of the jailor now knew no bounds. "*What! How!* Where!" he exclaimed, in broken ejaculations.

Fry's countenance grew darker as he clasped the old man in his arms, and said:

"We have stayed as long as we can stand it, and we now are going to leave, and let out the other prisoners; so give up the keys, and make no noise, or it will be the worse for you!"

Turner tightened his grasp on the keys desperately, and exclaimed, "You can't do that!" then commenced in a loud tone, "Guar...." when my hand closed across his mouth and stifled the incipient call for help.

It was not our intention to hurt the old man, for he had been kind to us; but it was necessary to keep him quiet. He possessed great strength, and struggled very hard, managing to bite my finger; but we held him fast, and easily wrestled the keys from him. Buffum was soon at work on the locks of the doors.

Meantime, our companions had quietly descended the stairway, and burst out on the guards. There were seven of them, but they were so much taken by surprise as to be incapable of resistance. Our boys divided into two parties, one for the front and the other for the back door. The latter was completely successful, capturing the guard, and taking their guns from them without the least alarm being given.

The attack at the front door was made with equal skill and bravery, and the guards who stood near were at once secured. Unfortunately there were two in the yard gate, which happened to be open. As soon as these saw the charge made, they, without waiting to attempt resistance, ran through the gate, shrieking, "Help! murder!" in tones that aroused the whole neighbourhood. There were troops near at hand, who instantly rushed to the rescue.

Our boys saw their peril, and knew that the part of our scheme which provided for a regular and quiet departure was defeated, and they endeavoured to save themselves. They threw away the guns, which now would only hinder their flight, and scaled the wall, some ten feet in height, and made for the woods, nearly a mile distant. It was a close chase. Several times they were fired on by the pursuing rebels, but fortunately not hit.

We, who were above, heard the noise, and were admonished by it to take our leave as soon as possible. Buffum had just succeeded in unlocking the door that kept in our other soldiers, who at once came out. The deserter confined with them, who was the most powerful and active of the whole party, also broke out, and passed by where Fry and myself still held the jailor, like a tiger on the leap. When he reached the yard, he found two soldiers before him, with their bayonets at a charge. Without a moment's hesitation, he seized them, cutting his hands severely, but dashing them aside with such violence as nearly to throw the rebels from their feet, and bounded on his way. His almost incredible swiftness soon placed him in advance of all the fugitives.

Captain Fry and I started down stairs together. He was a little in advance, and at once saw there was no chance in the front yard, which was now filled with armed rebels, and darted to the back door. Here he scaled the wall just in time to get away, after a most desperate chase, being repeatedly fired upon by the guards, who were only a few feet from him, but, fortunately, was unharmed.

I did not so soon comprehend the state of affairs, (probably because I am near-sighted,) and rushed to the front yard. Here I saw two rebels who seemed perfectly distracted, and were throwing their guns wildly about and exclaiming: "What shall we do? O! what shall we do?" Not thinking them very dangerous, I darted past them, but was checked by a stream of less frightened guards pouring through the gate. Seeing then that there was no chance of escape in that direction, I turned and regained the jail. One man snapped his gun at me, but, fortunately, it did not go off. I instantly tried the back yard, and succeeded in getting to the top of the wall; but here I found that the rebels had again been too fast for me, and were around under the wall outside. Under these circumstances, I could do no better than surrender.

I was taken back to prison, and instead of going to my own room, went to that occupied by the prisoners of war, who had all been recaptured and put in again. Buffum, too, who had managed to get over the wall, was retaken and brought back. Parrott and Reddick were captured inside of the wall, and Mason and Bensinger the next day, making six of our party who were retaken.

From the window where I was, I had a good view of all the proceedings below. In a very short time, the whole force of the place, including a regiment of cavalry, was drawn up in front of the jail. I heard Colonel Lee, (the Provost-Marshal,) give his orders. He said:

"Don't take one of the villains alive! Shoot them down, and let them lie in the woods for the birds and hogs to eat!"

He also ordered pickets to be placed at the ferries of the Chattahoochee, along the railroad, and at all cross-roads. This arrangement pleased me, for these were the very places we had agreed to avoid, and I was sure none of the boys would be caught there. Our intention had been to travel in the night time, through the woods, and cross the rivers on logs, as far from the ferries as possible.

Eight escaped. Wood and Wilson travelled southward, and, after passing through a series of the most startling adventures, that recall the old Indian tales we have all listened to in the winter evenings, they succeeded in reaching the Gulf, where they were taken on board a United States ship, and brought around to Washington.

Porter and Wollam started westward. Their journey was a most perilous one. I will insert a short account which Porter has since furnished me.

"We started on the 16th of October, and reached the Federal lines on the 18th of November. During this time, we endured all the hardships imaginable. We travelled night and day, sleeping mostly in the woods, and subsisting on wild grapes, chestnuts, hickory-nuts, walnuts, and some few sweet potatoes. Occasionally, we got a little corn-bread from the poor class of whites and the negroes. It was miserable stuff. Several times we slipped into the fields where the negroes were at work, and stole the provisions they had brought out for their dinner. Once we were seven days without a bite of bread, and often went without for two or three days.

"We suffered much with cold, for our clothes were very poor. We slept but twice in houses during the whole journey. One night we travelled till we became chilled and weary; it was very late, and we were nearly frozen, when we fortunately discovered *a nest of hogs*. Immediately we routed them up, and, lying down in the warm retreat they had left, slept till morning!

"Many streams were in our way, which we were obliged to wade, or float across on logs. After twenty-two days of such privations, we reached the Tennessee river, twenty-seven miles below Bridgeport. Here we pressed a canoe into the service, and started down the river. We would run the canoe at night, and hide it and ourselves in the day time. When we arrived at the head of the Muscle Shoals, we were compelled to abandon our canoe on account of low water, and make a circuit of forty miles around. When we reached the foot of the Shoals, we procured a skiff, and continued our voyage until within twelve miles of Pittsburg Landing. Here we left the river, and striking across the country to Corinth, reached there in safety. Thus, after six months of suffering, we were once more under the glorious flag of the free."

These[7] will serve as specimens of what the brave boys endured in the truly Herculean task of penetrating for hundreds of miles—in fact, from the very centre of the Confederacy to its circumference—in different directions. It is an achievement I can not look upon without wonder, and in dangers to be encountered, and difficulties to be overcome, is at least equal to the proudest exploits of Park or Livingstone!

All night long the guards talked over their adventures. Generally they praised their own bravery to the skies, but occasionally one who had arrived since the affray, would suggest that it was not very much to their credit to let unarmed men snatch their guns from them; but these hinted slanders were always received with the contempt they deserved, and the work of self-glorifying went on! One wondered at the speed of the Yankees, who had been kept in prison so long; another accounted for it by saying that they had received so much practice in that line, in all the battles they had fought, that it was no wonder if they were fleet of foot. This sally was received with prodigious applause.

I heard some confused sounds of distress from the room of the Tennesseeans, and on inquiring what was the matter, learned that Barlow had broken his ankle. He had gone down into the yard with our party, but in jumping from the wall, had received this very serious injury. Here he was found by a guard, who at first threatened to shoot him; but on being persuaded not to do that, ordered him to get up and lead the way into the jail. Barlow tried to do so, but fell down again. Then this inhuman guard punched him with the bayonet, and made him crawl, in all the agony that pain could produce, back to his cell, and as he went, kept hurrying him along by

---

7. Hawkins and myself associated, and made good our escape. We think all our party escaped to the woods. Whether any were afterward caught by the rebels, we know not. We travelled by starlight for more than three weeks. After twenty-one days of fatigue and hunger—living most of the time on corn or persimmons—occasionally a few raw sweet potatoes or a head of cabbage—dodging the rebel pickets and cavalry, climbing mountains, dragging through brush, and wading streams, we finally were so fortunate as to meet some Union men in the Cumberland Mountains. We met them, three in number, in the woods, and asked them to give us some supper, stating that we had no money, but we belonged to the rebel army, had been sick and left behind, and were now on our way to rejoin our regiments. They refused to supply our wants, and finally openly declared themselves to be Union men. When we became satisfied that they were all right, we made known our true character, and warmer friends were never met. They lodged and fed us, then piloted us to another Union man who did the same, and he to another; thus we were passed from one to another till we arrived at Somerset, Kentucky, where we procured transportation to our regiments.—*Extract from an Account published by D. A. Dorsey.*

the sharp admonition of the bayonet! When here, his companions asked for surgical aid for him, but the Confederate authorities refused it, saying that he had caused the injury himself, and that they rather preferred that it should kill him! Their wishes were gratified. For months he lingered on in the greatest pain, until, finally, the leg mortified, and terminated his life. He was quite a young man—only eighteen—and had just been married when he was arrested. Thus died, in darkness and dungeon, one other East Tennessee martyr!

Chapter 14

I Assist a US Spy to Escape

All night long I lay in the hammock that one of the regulars had swung by the window, and listened to the boasting below.

I had little doubt now, that the full weight of their vengeance would fall on every one who had been recaptured. And then, too, was the news we had received, and which had induced us to make our desperate effort to escape! We could scarcely hope that the death which had so long stared us in the face would now be longer delayed. And *such* a death! No vision of glory to dazzle the sight, and hide the grim monster from view, or wreathe him in flowers. No eye of friends beholding the last struggle, and sure, if you acted well your part, to tell it to those whose love and praise were more than life. Nothing but ignominy and an impenetrable darkness, beyond which no loving eye might ever pierce! But even as the cold horror of the scaffold and the vision of the heartless, jeering crowd, rose once more freshly before me, I looked out in the clear night, and up to the shining stars, and felt that I had one Friend—that He who dwelt above the stars, and to whom I had plighted my faith, would not forsake me, even if I had to pass through the very "valley of the shadow of death." With the thought came a still and heavenly peace once more—a peace that visits only those who feel, in the midst of sorrow and fear, that there is a blissful rest beyond the night bounding life's fleeting day!

The next morning, the jailor put me in the room I had formerly occupied, with the remainder of my companions. He told us that a man had put his hand over his mouth, and nearly smothered him, but added, with great satisfaction: "I bit his finger terribly, and gave the rascal a mark he will carry to the grave with him." However, his teeth were not so sharp as he thought, and he only managed to inflict a slight scratch. He had no suspicion that I was the person to whom he referred, as his fright had prevented him from observing anything. For a while, he was rather cross, and brought up the guards when he came to feed us; but this soon wore off.

About the middle of the day, some officers came, and, with many threats, asked us which way our boys intended to travel. I answered, "I heard them say that they were going to try to get to our lines, and that travelling in *any* direction would bring them there, for our men had you surrounded." They asked no more questions, but retired, satisfied that there was no information to be gained.

Our anticipations of worse treatment in consequence of our attempted escape were not realized. Colonel Lee thought the jail was no longer a safe place, and ordered us to be taken to the city barracks. Our apartment here was far more pleasant than our quarters in the jail had been. It was large, well lighted, and provided with a fire-place, which the chilliness of the days (it was now in October) made a great acquisition. It also commanded a view of one of the busiest public squares of Atlanta, and we would sit in the windows, which had no bars across them, and watch the tide of human life that flowed before us, for hours at a time, with an interest that only our long seclusion from the world could have given.

Jack Wells, the commander of the barracks, had been an old United States soldier. Being thus brought up under a more honourable system than obtains in the South at present, he did not consider it derogatory to his dignity to treat prisoners kindly. He would come around to our room and talk with us by the hour—telling us great stories of his adventures, and receiving as great in return. Most of the time he was half drunk, and very frequently did not stop at the half way point. In these cases, and when he was in a communicative mood, he would tell us that he did not care a cent which side whipped—that he only held his present position to avoid being conscripted. But his masters knew him to be such a faithful, vigilant officer, and he could so readily control the rude mass who occupied the rebel portion of the barracks, that they readily forgave these little slips of the tongue. We passed our time while here more pleasantly than at any other place in the Confederacy; yet even here, our path was not one of roses. The following incidents will prove this:

The Tennesseeans were confined with us, making twenty in all. Our provisions, which were still very scanty, were handed around in a tray. Mr. Pierce, who is mentioned before, one time conceived his allowance to be too small, and threw it back into the tray again. Not a word was spoken on either side; but in a few minutes the guards came up, and, seizing Pierce, took him out of the room into the cold hall, and tying his hands before his knees, with a stick inserted across under his knees and over his arms, in the way that soldiers call "bucking," they left him there all night. This indignity was perpetrated on an old man over sixty!

One of the guards was a malicious fellow, who delighted in teasing our men by asking them how they liked being shut up in a prison, "playing checkers with their noses on the windows," &c. One day, when he was talking as usual, a Tennesseean, named Barker, replied that *he* need not be so proud of it, for he would some time have to work like a slave, in the cotton-fields, to help pay the expenses of the war. The guard reported this *treasonable* remark to the commander. Poor Barker was seized and taken to the punishment-room up stairs, and there suspended by the heels till he fainted; then let down until he revived, then hung up again. This was continued till they were satisfied, when he was taken down, and put into a little, dark dungeon, only about four feet square, and there kept twenty-four hours with nothing to eat!

While in this prison, I had the heartfelt pleasure of helping one man to escape. The guards, and, indeed, all the poorer class of Southerners, were very illiterate. Out of twenty-six who guarded us, only two or three could write at all, and these not enough to be of any service. Wells wrote a hand that nobody but himself could read, and even he not always. Therefore he often came for the prisoners to write short articles for him. On one of these occasions I was in the office, which was just by our room, and equally guarded, writing a requisition for provisions. While thus engaged, a man, dressed in the uniform of a rebel officer, was brought in for confinement in the barracks. He appeared to be very drunk, but remonstrated so hard against being put into the room where the remainder of the prisoners were kept, that Wells consented to let him stay for a while in his office. His money was not taken from him, for Wells, not knowing the charge against him, believed he was arrested only for being drunk—an offence with which he had a good deal of sympathy. Wells had some business to attend to, and went out. A sergeant was with us, but he, too, soon took his departure, leaving us alone. I was busy writing, but, looking up, I saw the stranger approaching me. There was no trace of drunkenness about him. I watched his movements attentively. Soon he was standing by me.

"You are a prisoner?" he queried.

"Yes, sir."

"One they call engine-thieves?" he continued.

I again answered in the affirmative.

"I know you," said he; "I know all about you. I was here when your comrades were hung. Brave men they were, and the cruel deed will yet be avenged. I am not afraid to trust you. They don't yet know who I am, but they will learn to-morrow, and then, if I am still in their hands, I will *die*, for I am *a spy from the Federal army*. Can't you help me to escape?"

I was astonished at this revelation, and for a moment doubted his character, thinking that his aim might be to betray me for a selfish advantage. I put a few hasty questions to him, to test his knowledge of the Federal army. The answers were satisfactory, and seeing nothing but truth in his clear eye, I hesitated no longer, but asked:

"What can I do for you?"

He answered: "Can't you write me a pass, and sign the commander's name to it?"

"That," I returned, "would probably be detected; but I think I can put you on a better plan. Take that overcoat," pointing to one belonging to Wells, and lying on the foot of a bed, "put it around you, and just walk past the guards as independently as though you owned the entire establishment. It is now nearly dark, and the chances are that you will not be halted by the guard at all."

"A good idea," said he, "I'll try it."

At once folding himself in the coat, he bade me an affectionate adieu. Eagerly I sat with beating heart in the deepening twilight, listening for any sound that might betray the success or failure of the scheme; but all was silence. I have since learned that the guard, seeing the familiar coat, supposed that, of course, its owner was in it, and allowed it to pass unchallenged! A moment after, the sergeant came in, and I instantly engaged him in conversation, inducing him to tell some good stories, to keep him from missing my companion, and to allow as much time for a start as possible, before the inevitable alarm was given. I succeeded perfectly for some five minutes, when Wells came in, threw an uneasy glance around the room, and at once exclaimed:

"Sergeant, where is that officer?"

The sergeant protested that he knew nothing about him; that he was not in the room when he entered.

Wells then turned to me, and demanded:

"Pittenger, where's that officer?"

"What officer?"

"That officer I put in here."

"Oh! that drunken fellow?"

"Yes; where is he?"

"The last I saw of him, he picked up his coat, and said he was going to supper."[8]

"Going to supper, was he! Ho! I see it! Sergeant, run to the guards, and tell them if they let him out, I will have every one of them hung up by the heels."

This was rather a useless punishment, considering that the prisoner was already far away.

But the sergeant departed to muster the guards. Shortly after, Wells, who had resumed his seat, said in a meditative tone:

"Had he a coat?"

"I suppose so, sir," I returned, "or he would not have taken it."

"Where did he get it?"

"Off the foot of that bed."

Wells sprang to his feet as quickly as though he had been galvanized, kicking over the chair on which he had been sitting, and exclaimed:

"*My coat!* sure as——! Worth eighty dollars! The villain!" then pressing his head between his hands, sat down again, but, as if thinking better of it, ejaculated, "Well, if that ain't a cool joke!" and burst into a loud laugh, which ended the scene.

There are some facts connected with the Union sentiment in the South, which I would like to publish, if I dared; but I cannot do it in full, for it might be the means of exposing persons who befriended us, to the vengeance of the tyrant rebels. I will only say that there exists in Atlanta a society of over four hundred members,[9] who are still devoted to the cause of union and liberty; who endure in patient faith all the cruel persecutions heaped on them by the slavery-loving aristocrats who now rule their beautiful land. From members of this society many prisoners as well as myself, received money and other needed articles, which were of the greatest value to us. These were given at great risk to the donors, for *there* to give a Union soldier money is a serious criminal offence. One man I know was confined for four months on the mere suspicion of having aided the Shiloh prisoners in this manner.

Sweet potatoes were very abundant in Atlanta, and with the money Union friends supplied us, we bought a great many, roasting them

---

8. I do not pretend to justify the falsehoods recorded in this book. But it is better to give a *true* narrative, and bear the censure awarded by the reader, than to increase the guilt by omitting or misrepresenting facts.

9. My impression of Southern feeling is very different from Vallandigham's. But the Union men were my friends. Were they his?

in the ashes of the large fire-place that made our room so comfortable. They added materially to our rations, and rendered our living here more tolerable. In fact, had it not been for that universal Confederate pest, with which all, from the least to the greatest, seemed supplied—sometimes termed the "rebel body guard"—and from which, for the want of clean clothes, no exertions of ours could free ourselves, we might have passed our time not unpleasantly.

We still continued our devotions in the morning and evening, and trust that God blessed them to us. We met with occasional hindrances. Some of our own party seemed to consider that our release from the dark cells of a criminal prison did away with the necessity of continued prayer. The Confederates also annoyed us very much by interruptions, while thus engaged in seeking help from above. On these occasions, Wells was our friend. He declared that he could not stand praying himself, and so invariably stayed away; but that if it did us any good, we were welcome to it, and ought not to be disturbed. The opposition we met with was of short continuance. As soon as they found us firmly resolved on our own course, they did as all cavillers do in similar circumstances—let us alone. Thus even there we enjoyed many pleasant moments, which will ever be remembered as a green oasis in the parched desert of prison-life.

While here, the Confederates wanted some of us to enlist in their army. They tried particularly hard to get the regulars, Wells declaring that he would rather have the two, than any half dozen of his own men. They pretended not to be unfavourable to the scheme, but delayed complying with it for a time, to see what the ultimate prospects of an exchange might be.

The cartel of exchange had been agreed upon long before; yet these men, who had no charge against them, were still held. They believed that it was because they were with us, and that the rebels feared to let them go, as they would most certainly convey to our government intelligence as to our whereabouts, condition, and treatment. This view appeared still more probable, when I learned, since returning to Washington, that the Confederate government had *officially* denied hanging any of the party. They have never yet acknowledged it.

The time wore wearily away here, as it had done before. The delay, since the death of our friends, had now been so long extended, that we began to believe that our lives might be spared. This conviction was strengthened as the months rolled on. At last a court-martial was convened—the first since the ever-memorable one at Knoxville, and we awaited its action with the utmost anxiety.

A week of sickening suspense passed by, and no summons came for us. Then the court adjourned, and we breathed freer. It now seemed probable that they did not intend to prosecute the feeble remnant of our party any further; and, passing from the extreme of despair to that of hope, we began to indulge once more the blissful expectation of being permitted to revisit the scenes of our loved North, and stand beneath the "old flag," which we honoured and reverenced as the embodiment of liberty with law—the emblem of the highest national life. But our time for freedom had not yet come.

The weeks rolled on. Few things occurred worthy of note. That same monotony which makes prison-life so dreary, robs it of interest when recorded. We would rise in the morning from our hard bed, and wash ourselves, pouring the water upon each others' hands, and eat our scanty breakfast; then loll listlessly around, seeking in vain for anything which might relieve the almost unendurable tedium. When dinner came, which was of the same quality as the breakfast, we would eat it, and then try desperately to kill time until dark, when the gas was lit—not from any favour to us, but that the guard could watch us from the ever-open door, and see that we were working no plots to get out.

This was the most cheerful hour of the day, for under the soft inspiration of the gaslight, conversation flowed more freely, and all the incidents of our past lives were rehearsed to attentive listeners. To vary the subject, an argument would be started on science, politics, or religion, and warmly discussed. When the talk would flag, which was frequently not till the midnight bells were striking in the town, we would offer up our devotions, and lie down to sleep, and often to indulge in the most delightful dreams of freedom, friends, and home. In the morning we waked again, and the same round was recommenced. Thus days glided into weeks, and weeks passed into months. The light golden hues of autumn deepened into the dead and sombre colours of early winter, and still we were in Atlanta. Our weak faith, judging what would be from what had been, could scarcely conceive that we would ever be anywhere else! A heavy, dead indifference, like the lack of sensibility which the repeated infliction of pain produces in our physical natures, took possession of us. We almost ceased even to hope!

But at last there came a day of rejoicing. A number of officers visited the barracks, and inquired which was the room occupied by the Federal prisoners. On being shown around to our apartment, they told us to fall into line, and then said they had glad news for us.

"You have all been exchanged, and all that now remains is for us to send you out of our territory."

They then came along the lines, and shook hands with us, offering congratulations on the happy termination of our trials, and wishing us much joy on our arrival at home.

Our feelings may be better imagined than described. There was an overwhelming rush of emotions which forbade utterance—happy joy—exhilarating, and yet mingled with a deep touch of sorrow, that our seven dead—murdered—comrades were not with us to share the joy of this unexpected release. And the eight also who had managed to get out of the clutches of the rebels by their own daring—we were uneasy about them. Only a day or two before, we had seen in an Atlanta paper, obtained, as usual, through a *contraband* source, an article clipped from the *Cincinnati Commercial*, giving notice of the arrival of Porter and Wollam at Corinth, in a very wretched and famished condition. This was most gratifying to us, but of the others we had, as yet, received no reliable information. The Provost-marshal told us that three of them had been shot and left in the woods, but judging by the source, we considered the account very doubtful, and still cherished the hope that the whole story was a fabrication.[10] Thus we were in suspense as to their fate. But still, beyond all this, the prospect of speedily gaining our liberty, was enough to make our hearts overflow with gratitude to that Being who had so wonderfully preserved us through all our trials. I was so agitated that when Wells asked me to write a requisition for provisions for our journey, I could not do it, and had to transfer the task to more steady hands. It was six in the morning when we received the news, and we were to start for "home—*via* Richmond"—at seven in the evening. We spent the intervening time in arranging what clothes we had, and preparing for the journey. And as the time for departure drew near, we again lit the gas, and built a fire, the ruddy blaze of which was itself an emblem of cheerfulness, to take a farewell view of the room in which we had spent so many not altogether unhappy hours. Often afterward did we think of that bright hour of expectation, during the dreary lapse of succeeding months, which we were still doomed to pass in the South.

We had obtained quite a number of pieces of carpet, which served as blankets, but were forbidden to take these with us, being told that we would be run directly through, and would soon be where blankets

---

10. It was a malicious falsehood. All were safe.

were plenty. We however managed to secrete two very small pieces, which were afterwards of great advantage to us. They did not tie us now for the first time in all our travels. This was truly remarkable, and afforded strong confirmation to our hopes.

All was now in readiness for our departure, and we took a long, and, I trust, a last look at Atlanta—at least while it remains in rebel possession. The guards fell in on each side of us, and we wended our silent way along the dark streets. Wells, even drunker than usual, accompanied us to the cars, where he hiccoughed an affectionate farewell. White, the sergeant who was with me when our spy escaped, commanded our escort. He was one of the best-natured rebels I ever saw, and, like his superior, did not care which side came out best, so long as he was not hurt. The guard was only ten in number, while we, including the Tennesseeans, were twenty—a great falling off in precaution from their former custom.

We were crowded into rude box-cars, and soon began to suffer severely with the cold, for the night air was most piercing. It was the 3rd of December, and we had only summer clothing, which was, in addition, very ragged. At about three o'clock in the morning we arrived at Dalton. We were not to go through Chattanooga.

The stars were sparkling in light and frosty brilliancy when we stopped. The other train, on which we were to continue our journey, had not yet arrived, and the keen and icy wind cut almost through us. We stood shivering here, and suffering extremely from the cold, for something like an hour, when, to our great relief, the expected train arrived. We were more comfortably fixed in it, and managed to doze away the time till daybreak.

In the morning, we found that our three days rations, which were to last us to Richmond, were scarcely enough for a breakfast. However, we ate what we had, and trusted to buying a few necessaries with the remaining money which our Union friends had given us. When that failed, we had still a sure resource that never failed—endurance of hunger.

During the day, we discussed the question whether it would not be best, at nightfall, to try making our escape, as we were within forty miles of our own lines. It would be an easy task. The guards were perfectly careless, and at any time we could have had as many guns as they had. They sat on the same seats with us, and slept. Frequently those guarding the doors would fall asleep, and we would wake them as the corporal came around, thus saving them from punishment. The most complete security seemed to pervade them, utterly forbidding the idea that *they* thought they were taking us onward for any other purpose than that of exchange. Once the sergeant laughingly told us that we could escape if we wished, for we had the matter in our own hands; but that he thought it would be more pleasant to ride on around, than to walk across on our own responsibility. This very security lulled our suspicions, and, combined with what the Marshal and other officers had told us in Atlanta, induced us to shrink from undertaking a journey, almost naked and barefoot as some of us were, over the mountains and in the snow, which now began to appear.

In the afternoon, we passed the town of Knoxville, now a place of loathing and hatred to us; then the town of Greenville, which we noticed as being the residence of our heroic companion, Captain Fry; then on into the lower part of Western Virginia. It was nightfall when we entered this State, and a beautiful night it was. The moon shone over the pale, cold hills with a mellow, silver radiance, which made the whole landscape enchanting. On, on, we glided, over hill and plain, at the dead of night, and saw, in the shifting scenery of the unreal-looking panorama without, a representation of the fleeting visions of life—like us, now lost in some dark, gloomy wood, or walled in by the encroaching mountain side, and now catching a magnificent view of undulating landscapes, far away in the shadowy distance. Thus, through the silent night, we journeyed on, and morning dawned on us, still steaming through the romantic valleys of Virginia.

The next day was a wet, dreary one. Our car leaked, our fire went out, and we were most thoroughly uncomfortable. The evening found us at the mountain city of Lynchburg, which is literally "set on a hill." Here we discovered that we had missed the connection, and would have to wait for twenty-four hours. We were very sorry for this, as we were in a great hurry to get to our own lines, and had been talking all the way about what we should do when we arrived at Washington. But there was no help for it, and we marched up to the barracks with as good grace as possible.

We here found a large, empty-looking room, with some of the refuse of the Confederate army in it. There was an immense stove in the centre of the room, but, being without fire, it was of no particular benefit. We resigned ourselves to another night of freezing, with the consoling thought that we would not have many more of such to endure. I paced the floor till nearly morning, and witnessed a good many amusing incidents. Many of the Confederates were quite drunk, and disposed to be mischievous. One of them diverted himself by walking about on the forms of those who were trying to sleep. Soon he came around to Bensinger. He endured the infliction patiently the first time;

but as the sot came again, Bensinger was on the look-out, and, springing to his feet, gave him a blow that laid him out on the floor. Some of his companions rushed forward to resent the infliction; but, finding that nobody was frightened, they gave over.

Here, in Virginia, I met the most spiteful and venomous secessionists I had yet seen.

One of them—a prisoner—said that he had advocated raising the black flag, asserting that if it "had been done at first, the war would have been over long since."

"No doubt of it," I replied; "the whole Southern race would have been exterminated long before this."

This way of ending the war had not entered his mind, and he became very indignant at the suggestion.

All the next day was cold and gloomy. After noon, we succeeded in obtaining some wood for the big stove, with permission to make a fire in it, which was soon done, and a genial glow diffused over the whole room, in time to warm us before taking our departure for Richmond.

We started a while before dark, seated in good, comfortable cars—the best we enjoyed on the route. But we only ran a short distance to a junction, where we were again to change cars. The next train had not yet arrived, and we built a large fire, as it still continued bitterly cold. We could easily have escaped, for the passengers mingled with us around the fire, and we even went to a considerable distance away to procure fuel. But so confident were we of a speedy exchange, that we did not make the effort, and the golden opportunity passed unimproved. Oh! how greatly we afterward regretted that we had not at least made the attempt. Soon the other train arrived, and a few hours placed us in Richmond—the goal to which every Union soldier is turning his eyes, though he would not wish to reach it in the manner we did.

CHAPTER 15

Transported to the Rebel Capital

It was still the same sparkling moonlight, and the same intense and piercing cold, that marked our journey the preceding night, when we left the cars, and entered the rebel capital.

Everything looked grim and silent through the frosty air, and our teeth chattered fast and loud as we walked through a few squares of this now historic city.

But suddenly the sergeant recollected that he did not know what to do with us, and we were obliged to remain where we were, till he could find the Provost-Marshal's office, and get instructions. We endeavoured to shelter ourselves as best we could from the unbearable cold, which really threatened to prove fatal. We had two blankets, or rather pieces of carpet, and we spread them over the heads of us all as we huddled together in a solid mass, in the angle of a brick wall. It was astonishing how much more comfortable this made us—especially in the inside of the *pack*, where I happened to be. Here we remained shivering till the sergeant returned. He had found the Provost-Marshal's office, and proceeded to conduct us thither.

We marched through several of the principal streets, which, but for the moonlight, would have been entirely dark. At last we arrived at the office, which, to add to our discomfort, was destitute of fire. We stood in the empty room looking at the grim portraits of the rebel generals that stared at us from the walls, until the Marshal himself entered. He did not deign to speak to us, but opened a sealed letter which the sergeant handed him, and read that ten disloyal Tennesseeans, four prisoners of war, and *six engine-thieves*, were hereby forwarded to Richmond, by order of General Beauregard. We had hoped that the title of thieves, of which we had become heartily tired, would now be left behind; but it seemed still to cling to us, and afforded an unpleasant premonition of the

Confederacy's not yet being done with us. The Marshal then gave his orders, and we were again marched off.

By this time it was daylight, December 7th, 1862. Richmond looked still more cheerless by the cold beams of morning than it did before.

We now threaded several tedious streets, and at last came to the James river, where we halted in front of a most desolate-looking, but very large brick building, situated on the bank, and surrounded by a formidable circle of guards. This building we very naturally took to be a prison, and soon learned that we were right. It was the famous *Libby*. We entered its precincts, and were conducted up a flight of stairs, and then, on reaching the upper room, which was a vast, open one, we saw, almost for the first time since our capture, the old familiar United States uniform. We were soon in the midst of over a hundred Union soldiers.

At first our greeting was not very warm, as we still wore the rebel rags that had served us all summer; but as soon as our true character and history were made known, we were most cordially welcomed. There was a small stove—only one—in the cold, empty room, and part of the inmates were huddled around it. But with the characteristic courtesy and charity of the American soldier, they soon cleared a place beside it for us. Then I had leisure to look around.

The room was very large and bare; the floor above was taken out, leaving it open to the roof. Beside this, the window sashes were all removed, and the cold wind whistled in from the river far more sharply than was consistent with comfort. The inmates informed me that they had only a limited amount of fuel allowed them per day, and when that was exhausted, they had to endure the freezing as best they could. Even when the fire was burning, only about a dozen could get around it, and the room was too large and open to be warmed more than a few feet from the stove. Yet, with all these discomforts, we rejoiced to be here. It was the sure pledge that our foes had not been deceiving us in their promises of an exchange, for these men, with whom we found ourselves, were actually going northward in the next truce-boat, which was daily expected. Our hearts beat high as we thought that, after drinking the bitter draught of bondage and persecution for eight long months, we were at last to taste the sweets of liberty. What wonder if our joy was too deep for words, and we could only turn it over in our minds, and tremble lest it should prove too delightful to be realized! What cared we for the cold that made our teeth chatter, and sent the icy chill to our very bones! It was only for the moment, and beyond that we painted the bright vision of freedom, with such vividness and warmth, that cold and privations were forgotten together. But our dream was short.

We talked with our companions, and learned from them many interesting items of news. The worst we heard, and which, at first, we could hardly credit, was the existence of a large party in the North who were opposed to the war; because, as my informant said, "They were afraid if the thing went on, they would be drafted, and would have to fight themselves." Oh! how bitterly some of the prisoners, who were profanely inclined, cursed those who could oppose their government in such a time as this! Not many of the soldiers sympathized with these traitors. They were still hopeful of success, and confident that the time would soon come when they would crush rebellion.

But in the midst of our conversation, an officer entered, and called for the men who had just been admitted. Expecting to be paroled, as all the other prisoners in the room were, we at once responded. They conducted us down to the entrance hall, and called over our names. The four prisoners of war, and one of the Tennesseeans, were put on one side, and we on the other. The first party were then taken up stairs again, while we were put into an immense, but dark and low room, on the left of the stairway.

This was an awful moment. We now felt that we had been deceived, and our hopes at once fell from the highest heaven, to which they had soared, down to perfect nothingness, and a cold sense of misery and despair came over us. To be thus separated from our friends, also, seemed like parting the sheep from the goats, and could only be for the purpose of punishment! No wonder that we looked at each other with pale, troubled countenances, and asked questions which none were prepared to solve. But only one moment were we thus crushed beneath this unexpected blow; the next, we again sought an avenue for hope.

Perhaps they did not recognize us as soldiers, and only wanted to exchange us as citizens—a matter of indifference to us, provided we were exchanged at all. We looked around to see what foundation there might be for this pleasing conjecture.

Our present apartment contained even more prisoners than the one up-stairs. They were men from all parts of the South. Some of them had been in prison ever since the war broke out, and a few had been arrested for supposed anti-slavery principles, even before that event, and had lived in loathsome dungeons ever since. This would be called barbarous tyranny if it occurred in Italy; but I have seen men, even in my own Ohio, who could see no wrong in it when practiced in the South, on supposed *abolitionists*. There were also some of our own soldiers here, who had been put in for attempting to escape. This survey was not calculated to increase our feeble hopes of a speedy exchange, or even to weaken our fears of further punishment.

In the meantime, breakfast was brought in. It consisted of a small quantity of thin soup, and a very scanty allowance of bread. To our delight, the latter was made of flour, instead of corn meal; and all the time we remained in Richmond, we received good bread, though often very deficient in quantity.

While we were talking with our new room-mates, an officer again entered, and inquired for the fifteen men who had last come in. We answered quickly, for hope was again busy whispering in our hearts, and suggesting that there had been some mistake, which would now be rectified, and we taken up stairs again. But there was no such good fortune in store for us. We were taken out of doors, and there found a guard waiting to remove us to another prison. Again our hearts sank within us.

We crossed the street, and halted at a desolate-looking building, which we afterward learned was Castle Thunder, the far-famed Bastille of the South. We were conducted through a guarded door into the reception-room, where we had to wait for some time. While here, a fierce-looking, black-whiskered man, who, I afterwards learned, was Chillis, the commissary of the prison, came in, and said:

"Bridge burners, are they! They ought to be hung, every man of them; and so ought every man that does anything against the Confederacy." Had he said *for*, I would have agreed with him heartily.

Soon the guide returned, and ordered us to be conducted up stairs. Up we went, passing by a room filled with a howling and yelling multitude, who made such an outrageous racket that I was compelled to put my hands to my ears. As we came in view, a score of voices screamed with all the energy their lungs could give:

"Fresh fish! Fresh fish!" The same exclamation greeted every new arrival.

We were taken into the office and searched, to see if we possessed anything contraband, or, in plainer terms, anything they could make useful to themselves. They took some nice pocket knives from the Tennesseeans, which they had contrived to keep secreted till now. When it came my turn, I managed to slip a large knife, that I had obtained at Atlanta, up my sleeve, and by carefully turning my arm when they felt for concealed weapons, succeeded in keeping it out of the way.

The examination over, I thought they were going to put us into the miniature mad-house we had just passed; and they did not do much better, for they put us into a stall beside it. I call it a stall, for the word describes it most fully. It was one of a range, partitioned off from the large room in which were the noisy miscreants, and from each other by loose plank, with cracks wide enough to let the wind circulate freely through them. Most of the windows of the large room were out, which greatly increased the cold. Our stall was only eight or nine feet wide, and perhaps sixteen in length. It was bare of any furniture—not even having a chair, or any means of making a fire.

In this cheerless place our party, six in number, and nine Tennesseeans, were confined during the months of December and January!

The first day of our imprisonment here, our spirits sank lower than they had ever done before. All our bright hopes were dashed to the ground, and there seemed every reason to believe that we were doomed to this dreary abode for the remaining term of the war, even if we escaped sharing with our murdered friends the horrors of a Southern scaffold. It was too disheartening for philosophy, and that day was one of the blackest gloom. We seldom spoke, and when we did, it was to denounce our folly, in suffering ourselves to be deluded to Richmond by the lies they had told, and not seizing some of the many opportunities our journey afforded for making our escape. But it was no use lamenting; and all we could do was to register a solemn vow never to be deceived by them again. When night came, we knelt in prayer to God, and if I ever prayed with fervour, it was in this hour of disappointment and dread. I tried to roll all my cares upon the Lord, and partly succeeded, rising from my knees comforted, and assured that whatever might be the issue, we had one Friend who was nigh to save, and had often made his children rejoice, in worse situations than ours. The next morning I awoke again cheerful, and felt nerved for any fate that might befall me.

Here the routine of prison life did not differ materially from that at Atlanta. We had to go down to the court (the building was square, and built with an open court in the centre) to wash in the morning, and were immediately taken back to our stall, and locked up. But the principal difference was our want of fire. This made it our greatest difficulty to keep warm, and effectually destroyed all those pleasant fireside chats that had done so much to make our condition endurable in the Atlanta barracks.

As the darkness and coldness of night drew on, we were compelled to pace the floor, trying to keep warm; and when sleep became a necessity, we would all pile down in a huddle, as pigs sometimes do, and spread over us the thin protection of our two bits of carpet. Thus we would lie until too cold to remain longer, and then arise and resume our walk. We had always plenty of light, except when the awkwardness of the gas managers left the whole city in darkness, which was frequently the case.

We never omitted our devotions. For awhile the deserters outside, who were composed of the very scum of Southern society, many of them being the rowdies, gamblers, and cutthroats of the large cities, tried to interrupt us by every means in their power; but finding that their efforts produced no effect, they finally gave over, and left us to pursue our own way in peace. We found afterward, when, for a short time, we were put among them, that they respected us the more for it. Thus it will always be when perseverance is exercised in a good cause.

A few days after our arrival, we noticed a great stir among the prisoners at the Libby, which was plainly in view across the road, and but a short distance from us. We learned that a truce-boat had arrived. Soon a body of United States soldiers came up the street by us, and our five friends with them. As they passed our window, they waved their hands in farewell, and continued their journey. No doubt they were soon with their friends at home.[11] The parting was a hard one for us. It seemed so much like fulfilling the passage of Scripture—"One shall be taken and the other left," that we turned away from the window feeling again the gloom which darkened the first day of our arrival. We felt utterly deserted and alone; yet we were glad that some had been able to escape from the power of this accursed rebellion, "every throb of whose life is a crime against the very race to which we belong."

In the dead sameness which now settled down again over our prison-life, we had a delightful daily oasis, in reading the newspapers. In Richmond we were not, as elsewhere, debarred their perusal, and there was always some one who had money enough to buy them, and then charity enough to lend them all over the prison. In this way, we were enabled to see most of the dailies published. As soon as we received one, all the party would gather around, while I read the news and editorials aloud.

The time of our arrival was an exciting one. Burnside had just made his celebrated advance, and as we read of his crossing the river,

---

11. A letter was received from one of them by my father a short time ago. He had not heard of our release, but described our parting, and gave a rumour which he had heard of our subsequent execution.

we breathed a prayer that he would be successful, and continue onward to Richmond. Had he done so, we would either have fallen into his hands or been removed. In the latter case, we would have made a desperate effort to escape, for we had firmly resolved never to be moved again without making a strike for freedom.

But soon came the sad news of his repulse—sad to us, but causing the greatest rejoicings among the rebels, who felt that they had escaped a great danger, and renewed the life of their tottering treason.

We missed the books we were no longer able to borrow, and planned all kinds of means to obtain them. Among other expedients, I managed to sell my hat. It was a fine one, and had formerly belonged to Jack Wells; but one day when he was drunk enough to be in a clever humour, he took mine, which was a very poor one, from me, and put his own on my head, saying that I looked better in that. No doubt he intended to trade back, but forgot it when we started away, and so left me in possession. I sold this hat for three dollars and a half, and bought another extremely poor one for half a dollar, leaving me three dollars of available funds; which, added to five more afterward obtained from a Union man, made quite a fortune. With this I tried to procure a book I wanted. I gave the money to the corporal who attended the prison, but he kept it several days, and then returned it to me. I next tried one of the officers of the prison, but met with no better success. Determined not to be baffled, I dropped the money through a crack in the floor to a lady prisoner below, who was allowed to go out in town, but in a few days she, too, sent it back, saying that the book was not in Richmond.

Still persevering, I wrote the names of several books on a slip of paper, and gave it to Chillis, the commissary, who wanted us hung when we first came, but who was, nevertheless, the kindest official of the prison; he likewise returned it, saying that *none* of the books named were to be found. I then yielded, and reserved my money for the next best purpose to which it could be applied—to buy bread, which I often needed. We could at first get small cakes for ten cents apiece; but they afterward rose to fifteen. We had to take postage stamps in change, and, having no pocket-book to carry them in, they would often become torn and cracked, which rendered them worthless. Thus we lost a considerable portion of our precious money.

We soon became very restless and discontented here, and revolved desperate plans of escape. It seemed like a hopeless prospect, for we were in the third story, and could only escape by passing at each door through successive relays of guards, all of which had a reserve ready to cooperate with them in case of alarm. Our room was next to the jailor's office, and on the opposite side was a row of rooms containing all kinds of prisoners. The one next to us was occupied by a number of Federal soldiers—some charged with being spies, and others with murder.

One of the latter was Captain Webster. He was a young and most handsome man, not over twenty-two years of age. He had, on one occasion, been sent to take a notorious guerrilla captain, named Simpson, who was then hiding within our lines. When he was found, Webster summoned him to surrender. Instead of doing so he fired his pistol and started to run; but Webster also fired, and mortally wounded him.

When Webster was subsequently taken prisoner, he was held for the *murder* of Simpson, and confined in the room next to us. The charge I have repeatedly heard, not only from himself and fellow prisoners, but from the officers of the prison. Judge of my surprise, then, on reading, since my return home, of the hanging of Webster for *violating his parole*. This being a charge that the law of war would visit with death, the Confederates *officially lied* in substituting the one charge for the other, in order to justify themselves, and prevent retaliation.

Webster, too, was tired of confinement, and ready to risk all in a bold strike for freedom. The decision was soon made, and Christmas evening was the time fixed for the attempt. There were a number of citizens in the room below, who were in a more favourable situation for initiating the movement than we were. We had opened telegraphic communication, as we had done before at Atlanta, and after full consultation, it was agreed to let these citizens give the signal. This was to be the cry of fire, and when it was heard, we were all to rush upon the guards, and overpower them. There were only about thirty guards in the building, and we had over a hundred and fifty men concerned in the plot. We were, therefore, sure of success if every one performed his part—at least in getting out of the building, which was a less difficult task than leaving the city.

On Christmas eve everything was in readiness with us, and most anxiously did we wait for the signal. The hours rolled slowly on, and midnight passed, but no signal was given. We afterward learned that the citizens below failed in courage when the decisive moment came, and thus defeated a plan which would, in all probability, have been successful, and would have startled rebeldom no little in thus bursting open their strongest prison.

The next night we resolved to try once more. And that no faint-heartedness might now interfere, we appointed Webster our leader, knowing that he would not falter. Again we prepared. The locks of all the rooms were drawn except our own, which was so close to the guard that it could not be taken off without great danger of discovery.

Some did not want to go, but were very kind to those of us who did, supplying us with serviceable shoes, and taking our worn-out ones in return. At last everything being in readiness, we again waited for the signal. Those in our room were to remain quiet till it was given, and then burst off the door, which was a light one, and rush on the guard. We took a board that supported the water-bucket, and four of us, holding it as a battering-ram, did not doubt our ability to dash the door into the middle of the large room, and seize the guard before he could make up his mind as to the nature of the assault.

The other small rooms were soon vacated, the movement being concealed from the observation of the guard, by the inmates of the large room, into which all the others opened, standing up around the doors.

For an instant all was silence. We lifted up our hearts in prayer to God, that He would be with us, and preserve us through the coming strife, and if consistent with His high will, permit us to regain our liberty.

What can cause the delay? Minute after minute passes, and the dead silence is only broken by the throbbing of our own hearts. We stand with the board ready, and our spirits eager for the coming contest, which shall lead us to grapple, with naked arms, the shining bayonets of the guards. We do not doubt the issue, for the hope of liberty inspires us.

But now we see our friends creeping *back to their rooms!* We grind our teeth with rage and chagrin, but soon hear the explanation, which makes us think that the Lord is indeed watching over us.

Just as our leader was ready to give the signal, a friend pressed to his side, and informed him that we were betrayed, and that an extra guard of over eighty men was drawn up in line before the door, with orders to shoot down every one that issued from it, while still another detachment was ready to close in behind, and make an indiscriminate massacre. Had we attempted to carry out our plan, the guard would have yielded before us until we were drawn into the trap, and then they hoped to make such a slaughter as would be a perpetual warning to prison-breakers.

When I first heard this story, I thought it the invention of some weak-nerved individual who feared the trial and the danger of our scheme. But it was true. The next day the Richmond papers contained a full *expose* of the whole affair, and Captain Alexander, the tyrant who commanded the prison, threatened to have every one engaged in it tied up and whipped. But he finally concluded not to do so, and the excitement passed away.

Chapter 16
An Exchange is Proposed

All of our party had repeatedly tried to send letters home to let our friends know that we were still alive, but hitherto had failed. Now we had a providential opportunity. Some of the prisoners who were captured at the battle of Murfreesboro' were brought to Richmond, and confined in the basement of our building. While they remained, I wrote a note with a pencil, on the fly-leaf of a book, and when taken down to wash in the morning, slipped around to the door of the Western prisoners, and gave it to an Irishman. He concealed it until he was exchanged, and then mailed it to my father. It produced a great sensation among my friends, most of whom had long since given me up for dead. It was the first that had been heard of our party since the Atlanta escape, and was at once published in my county paper, and copied in many others. The following is the note:

Richmond, Va., January 6th, 1863.
Dear Father,
   I take the opportunity of writing by a paroled prisoner, to let you know that I am well, and doing as well as could be expected under the circumstances. I have seen some rather hard times, but the worst is past. Our lives are now safe, but we will be kept during the war, unless something lucky turns up for us. There are six of our original railroad party here yet. Seven were executed in June, and eight escaped in October.
   I stand the imprisonment pretty well. The worst of it is to hear of our men getting whipped so often. I hear all the news here; read three or four papers a day. I even know that Bingham was beat in the last election, for which I am very sorry.
   The price of everything here is awful. It costs thirty cents to

send a letter. This will account for my not writing to all my friends. Give my sincere love to them, and tell them to write to me.

You may write by leaving the letter unsealed, putting in nothing that will offend the Secesh, and directing to Castle Thunder, Richmond, Virginia. I want to know the private news—how many of my friends have fallen. Also tell who has been drafted in our neighbourhood, who married, and who like to be. Also if you have a gold dollar at hand, slip it into the letter—not more, as it might tempt the Secesh to *hook* it. I have tried to send word through to you several times before, but there is now a better chance of communicating since we came from Atlanta to Richmond.

No doubt you all would like to see me again, but let us have patience; many a better man than I am has suffered more, and many parents are mourning for their children without the hope of seeing them again. So keep your courage up, and do not be uneasy about me. Write as soon as you can, and tell all my friends to do the same.

Ever yours
William Pittenger
To Thomas Pittenger
New Somerset, Jefferson County, Ohio.

We remained in this prison, reading of the victories of Southern rebels, and the doings of Northern traitors, until the first of February. At that time they wanted our range of rooms for a hospital. This range was not adapted to the purpose, but was at least as good as the garret above, where all who went were sure of death.

Disease was now making fearful havoc. The small-pox prevailed to a frightful extent, and the whole town was alarmed. Men were dying around us every day; none of our party was infected, but many of the Tennesseeans were. It was no wonder that they found it necessary to extend their hospitals, for the treatment we received was well calculated to make the hardiest men sink beneath their trials. But these fearful ravages of pestilence did at least the good of securing our removal from the pen in which we had been confined. At first we were taken to the bedlam I have described before; and even this was better than the loneliness and *ennui* of our strict confinement.

It seemed like freedom by contrast. We now had a fire also—a luxury which one who has been *freezing* for two months knows well how to appreciate. It is true it did not warm half the people around it, and these had not the courtesy of our brethren in the Libby; yet it was a great thing to be occasionally warm.

The amusements of our new friends were striking, if not elegant. When a dense crowd would gather round the fire, some mischievous Irishman would cry out, "Char-rge, me boys;" and, with his confederates, rush against the mass, knocking men in all directions, upsetting pots, skinning elbows, and spoiling tempers generally. Fights were of frequent occurrence, and it only needed the addition of intoxicating liquor to constitute a perfect pandemonium.

The evenings were a compensation. After the turmoil of the day was over, and most of those who had blankets had retired to rest, a party of the worst rowdies, who had been annoying us all day, would gather around the stove, and appear in a new character—that of storytellers. I have spent the greater part of the night in listening to them, and have heard some of the finest fairy tales, and most romantic legends. But the approach of day put an end to all the romantic disposition of my companions, and left them ill ruffians as before.

We soon wearied of this perpetual ferment, and petitioned to be put below in the room with the Union men. After some delay it was granted, and then came a more pleasant part of my prison life. The room was large, but dark, and the windows not only secured by crossing bars, but woven over with wires. The refuse tobacco-stems of the manufactory had been thrown in this room, till they covered the floor to a depth of several inches.

But to compensate for these disagreeable accompaniments of our new apartment, it had a stove, and was warm; so that the terrible suffering with the cold, which none can appreciate but those who have endured, was now at an end. There was also good society here—nearly a hundred Union men from different parts of the South—all intensely patriotic, and many of them possessing great intelligence. In talking with these men, and hearing their adventures and opinions, I passed many a pleasant hour, and gained a great insight into the views of Southern Unionists.

One of these, who became an intimate friend, was a Scotchman, named Miller. When the war commenced, he was residing in Texas, and witnessed the manner in which that State was precipitated into secession. The first part of the plan was to excite rumours of a contemplated slave insurrection; then the conspirators would place poison and weapons in certain localities, and find them, as if by accident. This was continued till the public mind was in a perfect ferment. The next step was to take some slaves, and whip them until the torture made them confess their own guilt, and also implicate the leading opponents of secession. This was enough. The slaves and Unionists were hung together on the nearest tree, and all opposition to the nefarious schemes brutally crushed. Thus has slavery furnished the means of paving the way to treason!

Miller himself was taken, and after narrowly escaping the fate of his friends, was sent eastward to be tried as a traitor. He twice made his escape, once travelling over two hundred miles, and each time, when captured, telling a different story. Finally, he represented himself as a citizen from New York. When brought before Judge Baxter, the magistrate of Castle Thunder, for examination, he merely said:

"I told you all about my case before."

The judge, who was considerably intoxicated, thought that he had actually been examined before, and dismissed him without further questioning. He was brought up several times after that, but always gave them the same answer, thus keeping them completely deceived, and was at length exchanged.

I here became acquainted with a young man of the Potomac army, whom I shall call Charlie. He was employed to go near Richmond to fire a bridge, and collect important information. While executing his perilous mission, he was captured, with papers in his possession fully proving his character as a spy, and was despatched with a sergeant as escort, toward Richmond. While on the way, the sergeant, who was fond of liquor, got a chance to indulge, and became very careless. Charlie, watching his opportunity, slipped from the breast pocket of his guard the packet of papers containing his charges, with the directions for his disposal, and threw them into a pond by the wayside.

When he arrived at Richmond, the authorities did not know his character, and put him into the large room with the other prisoners, instead of confining him separately. When the evidence against him arrived, the commanding officer entered with a guard, and inquired for him. Now was his last chance for life, and well was it improved! It so happened that a man had died in the prison the night before, and Charlie at once responded:

"O! that fellow died last night," and pointed to the corpse.

"Died, has he! the rascal! We'd 'a hung him this week, and saved him the trouble if he'd only held on!" growled the officer, and departed.

Charlie was shortly after exchanged under the *dead man's name!*

Just when the discouragement of all lovers of their country was the greatest, resulting from the news of the rise and progress of the peace party in the North, a Tennessee Congressman visited our prison. He gathered the Tennesseeans around him, and urged them to return to their allegiance; stating that the Union cause was now hopeless, as it was abandoned even by the Northern States, which were in the hands of the Democrats, who would make peace on any terms; closing by asking them now to *do right*, take the oath of allegiance to the Confederacy, and go into its army, promising that all their previous obstinacy should be forgiven. The effect was wonderful! Listen, ye who cavil at the government, and while opposing its policy, still think you do no harm! These were loyal men, and had proved it by abandoning all for the cherished cause—many of them spending weary months in loathsome dungeons. Yet on hearing of the triumph of this faction, which promises to restore the Union by conciliating and wooing back the rebels, over one-half of them yielded, and gave that consent which neither danger nor suffering had been able to force from them! Thus were over twenty recruits from one room of one prison, obtained for the rebel army by the triumphs of Northern Democracy!

A part remained faithful, and this excited the ire of the secessionists. To punish them, Captain Alexander issued an order that all the menial service of the prison should be performed by Union men. Some obeyed the order, while others would not. But those who did the work complained that unwilling ones were not made to help them. To remedy this, a list was prepared, and the names taken in order. One of the first called was a Tennesseean, named McCoy. He answered boldly:

"I'm not going."

"What's the matter, now?" demanded the sergeant.

"I didn't come here to work; and if you can't board me without, you may send me home," replied the fearless man.

"Well! well! you'll be attended to," growled the sergeant, and proceeded with the roll. Four others likewise refused, and were reported to Captain Alexander, who at once ordered them to be put into "the cell." This was a dark place beside the open court, and only about four feet wide, by six or seven in length. It had no floor but the damp earth, and was destitute of light. Here they were informed that they should remain until they agreed to work.

We found another alternative for them.—There was a piece of file and a scrap of stove-pipe in our room, which we took, and buying a candle from the commissary, watched our opportunity, when taken out to wash, to slip them into the cell. As soon as these necessaries were received, the boys begun faithfully to dig their way out under the wall. All day and night they worked, but did not get through. The next day, we supplied them with another candle, and they laboured on. Toward morning, they broke upward through the crust of the ground outside. The foremost one wormed his way out, and glided off. He was never heard from, and no doubt reached the Union lines. The next man was just under the wall, when the barking of a dog, that happened to be prowling around, drew the attention of the guard that way, and prevented his escape. But though the stampede was thus arrested, it was a lesson that prevented the confinement of any more in the cell.

Yet they were not content to give up the idea of making us their servants. I happened to be on the next list prepared. This time the task was to dig in Captain Alexander's garden, which we would have been obliged to perform with an armed guard standing over us.

Of course, we refused to go. As a punishment, we were ordered into the yard, which was only a vacant corner of the building, enclosed by high brick walls, on the top of which guards walked. It was a cold day in February, and was raining. We were nearly naked, having only the remnant of the rags that had already served for more than their time. The bottoms were out of my shoes, and the water stood in the yard several inches deep. The cold, wet wind, swept down with biting sharpness, and almost robbed us of sensation. We paced the narrow bounds, through the mud and water, until too weary to walk any more, and then resigned ourselves to our misery!

Here we remained from early in the morning till in the evening. They told us we would have to stay there till we agreed to work, or froze to death! The first we resolved never to do. The latter was prevented by relief from an unexpected source.

The old commissary, who had been so harsh to us when we first arrived, now went to Captain Alexander, and remonstrated with him for his cruelty.

Said he, "If you want to kill the men, and I know the rascals deserve it, do it at once. Hanging is the best way. But don't keep them there to die by inches, for it will disgrace us all over the world."

This logic produced a good effect, and the order was given to send us back to our room, which, with its warm fire, never seemed more pleasant. It was well they did not keep us out during the night, for we had determined to scale the wall, if we lost half of our number in the attempt.

The effects of that terrible day of freezing were soon visible. On entering the room, the grateful warmth produced a stupor from which most of us awoke, sick. Some died. I, myself, contracted a disease of the lungs, which rendered me an invalid for months after regaining my freedom.

One day we were ordered into line, and the names of all our railroad party, with a few of the others, called over. One, whose name was omitted, asked the reason of the omission. The officer answered:

"We can't tell, for this list came from Yankee land."

The mention of "Yankee land" started conjectures afloat thick and fast. Why should a list be sent from the North? Could it be for the purpose of exchange? The whole prison was in a ferment.

They soon discovered that a general exchange of political prisoners was in contemplation. This added fuel to the flames. But as the truce-boats went off one after another, and week after week passed by, leaving us still in our dark and wearisome prison, hope again died away. Every person who ventured to speak of exchange was laughed into silence.

One day an officer came into the room, and ordered a sergeant to take the name of every man who claimed United States protection, in order to obtain clothes for him. Soon the clothing came. It did not comprise a complete suit, but was extremely welcome. Never did I see a peacock strut with more ostentation than did some of the prisoners on donning the uniform. And it was worthy of pride. It was a token that we were not forsaken, but that a great nation was extending its protection over us. The ragged guards around, clad in their miserable butternut suits, growled many uncomplimentary allusions to the penuriousness of their own government, in contrast with the munificence of ours.

There were only about one hundred *parts* of suits distributed, though the papers, the next day, stated the number at *five* hundred! and this I afterward found was actually the number sent from Washington. The entire four hundred, and part of the last hundred, was kept by the officers as a compensation for their trouble in distributing them! But they certainly acted with more than their ordinary honesty in giving us any at all!

On the evening of the 17th of March, when we were sitting around the fire, lazily, but not indifferently, discussing the siege of Vicksburg, and laying many infallible plans by which it might be at once reduced, an officer entered, and gave the strange order for all "who wanted to go to the *United States* to come to the office!"

When I obeyed, it was with very little hope that there was really a chance once more to stand beneath the folds of our loved banner. Even when part of our room-mates had gone in, and signed the oath of parole, I feared that the good news was *only* for them. To test the matter, I went forward, and as I gave my name, fully expected to hear—"The engine-thieves can't go"—but no objection was made.

For a moment a delicious hope thrilled through my veins—a vision of happiness and home, dazzling as a flash of summer lightning, shone before my eyes—but it instantly faded before the remembrance of our Atlanta deception.

It was announced that we were to start at four o'clock the next morning. The evening, as might be expected, was one of wild excitement. Nearly all acted like men bereft of reason. Their joyousness found vent in vociferous cheers—in dancing and bounding over the floor—in embracing each other, and pledging kind remembrances. But there were a few who were not permitted to go, and I pitied them. I remembered when we had been left by our comrades on our first arrival in Richmond, and my heart bled for these forsaken ones, as they sat cheerless and alone, seeming to feel even more wretched than ever, amid the general joy.

It was near midnight before we became calm enough to offer up our usual evening devotions. But when all were at length still, wearied out by the very excess of joy, and when the quietness that ever follows overwhelming emotions had settled down upon us, we knelt in prayer—a prayer of deep, strong, fervent thankfulness; and we implored that we might not be deceived in our bright and vivid hopes, and dashed back from our anticipated paradise; yet if such should be His high and mysterious will, and we should see these hopes fade, as others faded before them, we asked for strength to bear the trial. Thus composed, we laid down to sleep, and await the event.

Few eyes closed during the entire night. Fancy was too busy peopling her fairy landscapes—picturing the groups that awaited us beyond that boundary which, for nearly a year, frowned before us, gloomy and impassable as the silent river of death! But even as we muse, what unbidden fears spring up to darken the prospect, and stain the brightness of our joy! How many of those friends whose love was as our life, may be no more! For a year, not a whisper had been heard, and we trembled as we thought of the ravages of time and of battle. These and other thoughts whirled through our throbbing brains during that ever-memorable night, and were only broken by the summons of the commanding officer, who, long ere morning light, gave the thrilling order to—*prepare for our journey!*

Hurriedly we thronged to our feet. It was true! Freedom once more! Our terrible captivity was passed! O joy! Joy!—almost too wild and delirious for earth!

There was a hurrying around in the darkness illumined by the flashing of torch-lights—a discordant calling of names—a careful inspection to see that none went but those allowed; then, forming two lines in the courtyard, and with bounding hearts, we passed *outward* through the dreaded portals of Castle Thunder—the same portals we had passed *inward* more than three months before! passed out into the cool, but *free* night air!

We next marched through the muddy, unlighted streets for many squares. There were with us a number of sick, who were not willing to be left behind; and as the rebels refused to provide conveyances, we helped them—encircling them in our arms, and supporting their tottering steps during the weary distance. Some had to be carried altogether, but the burden was light, upborne, as we were, on the wings of hope and exultation.

After we were seated in the cars, we found in some Richmond papers the intelligence that "a large number of engine-thieves, bridge-burners, murderers, robbers, and traitors will leave this morning for the United States," also congratulating themselves on the riddance. Our congratulations were not less fervid!

We glided slowly along, passing fortifications and rifle-pits, till we arrived at Petersburg; then onward to City Point, the place of general exchange. Here, for the first time in eleven months, we saw the "flag of the free," floating in proud beauty from the truce-boat *State of Maine*. It was a glad sight! Her undulating stars were fairer to us than the brightest constellations that ever sparkled in the azure fields above.

The grossest frauds are often practised by the unscrupulous secessionists in these exchanges. I will give a case that occurred at this time.

A rebel soldier was wounded in the head at the first battle of Manassas. It affected his brain, and disordered his intellect, so that even after he had recovered physically, he was mentally unable to perform the duties of a soldier. He was confined a short time in Castle Thunder, and then sent to Camp Lee, to try him again. But he was no better than before, and they gave up the attempt in despair. Then they exchanged him to us, and got a *sound man* in his place!

When the boat rounded out from the shore on its homeward way, our joy knew no bounds. It seemed as if we had awakened from a hideous nightmare dream to find that all its shapes of horror and grinning fiends had passed away, and left us standing in the free sunlight once more. Our hearts beat glad music to the thresh of the wheels on the water, knowing that each ponderous stroke was placing a greater distance between us and our hated enemies.

Then, too, the happy welcome with which we were greeted; and the good cheer, so different from our miserable prison fare, and the kind faces, smiling all around, showed in living colours that we were freemen again.

Down the river we went, passing the historic ground of the James, as in a delirious dream of rapture! We were scarcely conscious of passing events. No emotion on earth has the same sweep and intensity as the wild, throbbing sensations that rush thick and fast through the bosom of the liberated captive!

On we went—reached the gunboats that ply up and down the river, like giant sentinels, guarding the avenue to rebellion—reached the river's mouth, passed onward up the bay to Washington! As we came in sight, we thronged tumultuously to the vessel's side, and bent eager, loving eyes on the snowy marble front, and white towering steeple of our nation's Capitol.

On our arrival, we were requested by the Secretary of War to give our depositions before Hon. Joseph Holt, Judge Advocate General, that the world at large might know on the surest foundation the truth of our narrative. We were received by the Judge himself, and Major-General Hitchcock, who was present, with the most marked cordiality. This interview was merely a friendly one, and was passed in familiar conversation.

On our second visit, we found a justice of the peace in waiting to administer the necessary oath, and also a phonographer to write our testimony. We were examined separately, and the result published officially in the *Army and Naval Gazette*, and also in most of the newspapers of the day.

We then called on the Secretary of War, accompanied by our kind friends, Major-General Hitchcock and J. C. Wetmore, Ohio State Agent. Generals Sigel and Stahl, with many other distinguished personages, were in waiting, but we were given the preference, and at once admitted.

The Secretary conversed with us most affably for some time. Then going into another room, he brought out *six medals*, and presented them to us, saying that they were the first ever given to private soldiers. Jacob Parrott, the boy who endured the terrible beating, received, as he well deserved, the first one.

He next presented us with one hundred dollars each, and ordered all arrearages to be paid, and the money and the value of the arms taken from us to be refunded.

This was not all. He requested Governor Todd to promote each of us to first lieutenants in the Ohio troops; and, if he failed to do so, promised to give us that grade in the regular army. We then received furloughs to visit our homes, and left his presence profoundly convinced that "republics are" not always "ungrateful."

We were then escorted by our friends to the Executive mansion, and had a most pleasing interview with our noble President. His kindness was equal to that of the Secretary. After relating to him some incidents of prison experience, and receiving his sympathizing comments, we took our leave.

And now—safe in a land of freedom—with the consciousness of having performed our duty—surrounded by fathers and mothers, brothers and sisters, wives and children, who had long mourned us as dead—our dangers past, and our sufferings rewarded—I drop the veil.

www.ingramcontent.com/pod-product-compliance
Lightning Source LLC
Chambersburg PA
CBHW021006090426
42738CB00007B/682